LOOSE UNITS

Paul F. Verhoeven is a writer, broadcaster and entertainer. A mainstay on the Australian media landscape, he has written for ABC News Online, *IGN*, *Smith Journal* and *Yen Magazine*, and has spent years working extensively as a games journalist. After beginning his career hosting *Weekend Breakfast* on Triple J, he went on to host and write *Steam Punks* on ABC TV, and currently co-hosts the critically acclaimed podcast 28 Plays Later.

LOOSE UNITS

Paul F Verhoeven

VIKING
an imprint of
PENGUIN BOOKS

The following is based on true events. In order to make this into a good read, some cases have been played with, stitched together, mashed into one another or blown apart for the sake of making them into actual tellable stories. Some names and locations have been changed to protect identities and organisations. Some stories told to the author were unfathomably threadbare, and the author was given permission to 'fill in the blanks carte blanche', which was initially vexing, especially as the author is convinced his father has no idea what 'carte blanche' means. All of these events happened, in short, but time has a way of playing with one's recollection of the specifics. The author's father would also like to apologise for the repeated references to *The Thorn Birds*.

VIKING

UK | USA | Canada | Ireland | Australia
India | New Zealand | South Africa | China

Penguin Books is part of the Penguin Random House group of companies whose addresses can be found at global.penguinrandomhouse.com.

First published by Penguin Random House Australia Pty Ltd, 2018

Text copyright © Paul F. Verhoeven, 2018

The moral right of the author has been asserted.

All rights reserved. Without limiting the rights under copyright reserved above, no part of this publication may be reproduced, stored in or introduced into a retrieval system, or transmitted, in any form or by any means (electronic, mechanical, photocopying, recording or otherwise), without the prior written permission of both the copyright owner and the above publisher of this book.

Cover design by Adam Laszczuk © Penguin Random House Australia Pty Ltd
Cover photograph by Bo Zaunders/Getty Images
Typeset in Adobe Garamond by Midland Typesetters, Australia
Printed and bound in Australia by Griffin Press, an accredited ISO AS/NZS 14001 Environmental Management Systems printer.

 A catalogue record for this book is available from the National Library of Australia

ISBN 978 0 14378 316 9

penguin.com.au

For my incredible mum, Christine, my flawless fiancée, Tegan, and my dad, John. Dad, you're a huge dork with zero attention span, but you're the best man I know.

Here's to many more adventures.

PROLOGUE

I was seven years old when I saw my first dead body.

It took me a moment to register what I was looking at. I distinctly remember feeling very sick, then very cold all over. The body was a woman's. Her eyes were still open, her pale hand was extended, and one of her legs was twisted under her body at a strange angle. Her blouse was torn, and there was a lot of blood.

At seven I was a small, skinny, generally cheerful kid. On this particular night I strayed from a dinner party my parents were throwing to go spelunking in a large walk-in closet at the back of our home. Before you get the wrong impression, there wasn't a body in the closet itself, this isn't going to be one of *those* stories. I'd simply reached an age where the length of my limbs, when splayed outwards, perfectly corresponded with the width of the closet. And given that I had unusually large feet and hands, and given that the walls had a certain degree of stick to them, and given that our ceilings were unreasonably high, it wasn't uncommon for me to wedge my arms outwards, Samson-style, and then shimmy up the walls until I was flush with the closet's ceiling.

The first time my parents came looking for me in there, with me pinned against the roof, and them standing directly underneath me with a puzzled innocence, I felt a sense of intense elation. I had suckers for hands and nothing could bring me down.

This giddy triumph was marred slightly after they left, when the sweat of adrenaline that had been collecting on my palms broke the bond between me and the walls, sending me plummeting, like a freshly felled Hans Gruber, down, down, down. And right onto a stack of boxes.

Though the option of a full ceiling wedge remained attractive, on this night it was these boxes I instead decided to dive headlong into, both figuratively and literally. The dinner party continued in the living room, with my parents making loud, muffled jokes. I'd brought a small flashlight with me, wanting to keep my presence covert. Even then I liked to imbue everything I did with a sense of needless intrigue. And the second I pulled the lid of the first box away, my flashlight beam fell upon a large, glossy black-and-white photo of a crime scene. It was of a woman's body. I took a moment to process what I was seeing. The body was upsetting, and I quickly shoved it away, not wanting to stare death in the face. There, I thought, I did it. The four-second rule at work.

But beneath the first photo was another. This one . . . this one had something wrong with it. There was a mass of blood in the centre of a room. Burnt fragments of hair and skin clung to the floorboards. I could see the feet of someone standing in the corner of the photo, presumably a police officer. Wordlessly I replaced the lid, snuck back to bed, turned off the lights and eventually drifted into unconsciousness.

My parents informed me the next morning that I'd been screaming in my sleep all night.

I didn't tell them what I'd seen.

The picture of the body bothered me, true. But the second picture seized me with a kind of existential dread. Because I didn't get a great look at it, and because I was coursing with adrenaline and looking at it in a poorly lit closet, it began to evolve. The photo was vague enough, and the memory of it hazy enough, for my mind to fill in the blanks with nightmarish details. Suddenly, every blank space, every spare corner of my growing mind was populated with blood, fear and death, and I began having night terrors on a regular basis. The photos weren't even that full-on, but my brain hadn't been exposed to anything violent or graphic up until this point; it was like an Amish youth on Rumspringa, one minute weaving baskets and whistling to itself, the next, doing ice in a wheelie bin. It was a violent gear-shift, and it completely knocked me off course.

When I was in my early teens, I relented and let my parents send me to a child shrink, to try to figure out why I couldn't stop screaming in my sleep. The shrink couldn't help, and I just accepted the now recurring dream as an immutable object, folding it into the architecture of my life. Which was totally fine, until as an adult I started a relationship with a woman who told me the dreams had to go, or she would. Snoring was one thing; screaming 'WHAT DOES THE BURN MEAN? WHY IS THE FLOOR BURNED? WHY IS THERE SO MUCH BLOOD!' was, evidently, another.

Perhaps those dreams are why I've ended up the way I have. I'm in my mid-thirties and I review video games for a living. I ended up studying film at uni and doing a lot of bad theatre, spent years as a presenter on Triple J, and have pretty much bounced between every weird artsy calling you can think of. Which is all well and good . . . but I mean, come on. Look at my dad. Hero cop.

And he *was* a hero cop – certainly to all the people he helped, the officers who ran alongside him, and to me, who sat there building Lego aberrations on the shag-pile carpet as he came home every day, resplendent in his uniform.

But the dreams have come back, and I'm thirty-five, and I'm looking at the genteel hipster fop I've become, and then I get this package in the mail. And it's full of photos of me as a baby, and I'm being held by my dad, unbelievably young, in his police uniform. Mum and Dad have decided to move overseas and in a newfound Zen-like purge are getting rid of keepsakes. So Mum bundled up sheaves of photos yellowed with age and sent them to me, which I pore over slowly in my office. And then, everything hits me. Why didn't I end up like him? Why couldn't I have adventures like he did? Why did I turn out so soft?

That photo.

It was that fucking photo.

So I call Dad and tell him we need to get to the bottom of this, once and for all – the case of why the apple fell so far from the tree. (Actually, that implies that I pursued a life of crime; it would be fairer to say that he became a man of action, whereas I avoided action at every turn.)

I needed him to break down why I hadn't turned out like him, and why I seemed built to baulk at the cruel truths of life, whereas he was apparently wired to face them head on, and without a whiff of retching. Dad and his partner, Julian – his best friend and the guy I called Uncle while growing up – were heroes to me. They ran towards conflict and action together. I worshipped them both. Why, then, did I struggle so much with conflict? Why did I enjoy the idea of adventure, but come over all reticent when the time came to actually charge at something head on? Why did I view everything through the prism of niche nerd references? Had something not been passed down from Dad to me during my birth? Had something been lost in translation? Did my paltry 'adventures' come anywhere close to his?

So I fill Dad in on my grievances, and after a pause, he asks if they'd wasted their money on the shrink. I inform him, yes, they most certainly had. The dreams were back. And when I confess how bothered I am that I'd not been able to bolt towards conflict and save lives, he sighs. Appalled I'd not come to him years before, he proposes something: saturation. He offers to share some of the darkest, most tangled, horrifying and strange stories I've ever heard, in the hope that they'll not just make the dream seem like a whisper by comparison, but so that I might understand why a photo – and that photo in particular – might not be so bad, after all. He tells me to trust him.

So that's exactly what I do.

My folks live in Beacon Hill, tucked away on the northern beaches. I hadn't been back in years, and had forgotten how dizzyingly weird the geography is there; it's practically Jurassic. Nestled in what is effectively a valley, surrounded by byzantine networks of architectural oddities, my parents' place hugs the hillside, squat, dark and legitimately mysterious. Everything there has a sense memory attached to it. That carpet? I threw up on that carpet. That windchime? I taped it once and worked the audio into a mixtape for a friend who has a pathological fear of windchimes. Once, halfway through listening, she almost crashed her car. Memories bubble up as I head around the side of the house, laptop and microphone in hand.

Mum hears my approach and runs to greet me. Mum is a brilliantly sunny woman, and she practically bounces ahead of me, yelling 'John! John!'

Dad yells back, sounding cheerful. I get a pat on the back from Mum, and she trots up to the kitchen. I head downstairs.

Picture a study: mahogany, leather, a faint fug of cigar smoke, and light perforated by venetian blinds. Fill the room with bookshelves, and fill those shelves with an inordinate number of Clive Cussler novels. Now, put my father on a leather armchair in the centre of the room, flanked by the same boxes I crash-landed on decades earlier, their lids still battered from the impact. The room has floorboards, with antique rugs laid over one another clumsily, and there's a window open. Dad always leaves a window open.

Now picture my dad, John. Tall, greying, stylish. He's a hair over six feet tall, broad shouldered, in his late fifties, calm and collected. And he maintains this air of cool right up until the moment I enter the room.

It is now that I clock his new reading glasses, which magnify his eyes to such cartoonish levels that I have to sit down on account of the laughter. Once I calm down, Dad pours me a glass of water and asks me where I want to begin.

I

DON'T BE A TOOL

John grew up in country New South Wales in a little town called Armidale. His family were old money, or so he was told; he often asked why it was, then, that they never seemed to have any. He never got a response that satisfied him. As far as I can tell, they were old money from way back, but eccentrics, and as such frittered it away.

His father and mother were schoolteachers and nonconformists. They imbued him therefore with a dual sense of hunger for knowledge and a need to be as weird and obtuse as possible. Eventually, they towed the family to Beacon Hill. John's family consisted almost entirely of strange people with even stranger personalities, like disgraced lawyers, experimental musicians and religious fanatics, which might be why he went in so many random directions with such fervour. John dropped out of high school in year ten, then dabbled as a skydiving instructor and a scuba diving instructor in his late teens before taking up toolmaking. But, as John was so fond of muttering to himself as he worked, 'making tools is for tools'. He was bored, tired, and lost.

And at the age of twenty, at the tail end of a terrible week working on the factory floor, John found himself hiding from his boss, squatting on a toilet. He'd locked the door and cinched his legs up. His shift had crawled on for ten hours. He was exhausted. The dinky, cramped outdoor cubicle at the back of the factory was the only place to get some breathing room.

A breeze stirred up, whipping some newspaper under the door. Looking to draw out his recess, John picked up the papers and began to peruse them. A large advertisement caught his eye, asking young people across the state – pleading with them, in fact – to join the police force. The advertisement prominently featured an attractive young cadet, gesturing towards a large logo, smiling dazzlingly at the camera.

John was squatting. He was hiding. He was tired. The young cadet on the pamphlet grinned irresistibly, alluringly.

'I have to meet her,' he whispered to himself.

It was that simple. John decided to enrol at the police academy and impulsively quit his toolmaking job. It didn't go down well with his family. The police had assaulted Aunt Frannie during anti-war protests in the seventies. She was an academic at the time and very politically active, and after she joined peaceful protesters and was punched repeatedly in the stomach by men in uniform, the whole family swiftly developed an almost allergic reaction to authority figures. When John came back home clutching the ad from the paper, claiming he'd made up his mind, it's fair to say the family went a tad dark.

But John was young and stubborn. He'd spent years trying to impress his folks, and then even more years trying not to. He grew up in the country and knew how to shoot, was adept at the trumpet, and could run a mile lightning-fast. He'd always wanted to get things done, and had hoped that he'd somehow win the approval of his parents doing so. But when that didn't work, he took to being a bit of a shit. And that didn't work either. Toolmaking wasn't what he wanted to do; he didn't know *what* he wanted to do. So when he saw the ad in the paper and was gripped, finally *gripped* by a sense of conviction and direction, by the notion that here was something he could actually *do*, he pushed his family baggage to one side. He left work and never looked back.

Actually, that's not fair. He didn't look back because his boss terrified him, and he was running as if his life depended on it. That night, he made some hushed calls and lined up an interview.

At nineteen, he was skinny. Too skinny. There were very specific physical prerequisites for acceptance into the police force. John made it through the initial test, but then was wheeled into a tiny room where he was poked, prodded and tested for flaws. If the lone doctor looming above him with a pencil behind his ear was a dock worker, he was the ship, and the doctor was checking for leaks. Then, he found one.

John's chest wasn't wide enough. He was a few centimetres short of greatness. He wasn't well built enough to qualify – 'scrawny' was the word the doctor used on the day.

Seeing the expression on John's face, the doctor leaned in and, under his breath, urged him to take a deep breath and puff his chest out. John did so, and to his dismay, he was still an inch short of the tape measure wound around him. After a moment, the doctor sighed, said, 'Close enough,' patted him on the back and emphatically stamped the form.

He was in. They'd had to bend the rules, but he was in.

That's fine, John thought. I mean, they're breaking the rules for me, but that's fine. I'm in. And then later, he wondered if it *was* fine. Eventually he decided it was, provided he got the job.

And he did. They accepted his application, and six months later, one cold morning in 1980, he fronted up to Redfern Police Academy. It was a looming red brick building, girt with immaculate lawns, and it looked like a private boys' boarding school. John headed in, handed over his paperwork, and just like that began training.

For two whole weeks, he and a slew of other prospects were run through some initiation, physical training, some light hectoring from instructors. Then John and the other recruits, their uniforms still crisp and clean, were shunted up to the fourth floor. They filed into a room filled with light blaring in through enormous windows. There was a window cleaner perched outside, smoking a cigarette. John made eye contact with the window cleaner for a moment; he looked back, bored. I could have been a window cleaner, John thought. That could have been me out there, working in a shit job. John wondered if he was jealous, or indifferent. Or if that was even tobacco.

The brass began drumming into the wide-eyed recruits the many different types of policing that came under the law enforcement umbrella of the New South Wales Police, things they might end up majoring in, effectively. Perhaps, they were told, you'll end up in traffic, or dog squad. Maybe the Air Wing. Undercover. Homicide, drugs, regional crime. Bikies. Organised crime squad. Internal affairs. Water police. You might end up working away in forensics. Or maybe you'll end up a detective. John's ears pricked up at the mention of detective. He liked the sound of that.

The desks were cheap. Formica. Dicks carved onto every available surface. The kind of flimsy classroom numbers that John grew up with in school in Armidale. His family, staunchly Catholic, sent him off each morning in the hope that he wouldn't come back home any morally scruffier than he was when he'd left.

Their hopes were for naught.

For it was he who carved the dicks.

Every day these young officers filed in, blinked on account of the blinding sunlight, pretended to ignore the clearly stoned window cleaner, then sat in the uncomfortably tiny chairs. It was uncannily like school. Instead of ultimately useless forays into arithmetic, John sat and heard about more detective work, forensic work, traffic, arson, whatever. He sat there, already beginning to toy with a possible career path.

John noticed that as he and his fellow recruits queued up for class in the corridor, other students would rush past on their way to more interesting destinations. Some of them had placements. Some were in trouble, and were either running towards or away from that trouble. And every morning, a young, beautiful woman would walk past with purpose down the hallway. It was the woman from the flyer. John, it's safe to say, swooned.

> I raise an eyebrow. 'Are you telling me you joined the force because you had the hots for the girl on the flyer? Or because you wanted do something meaningful with your life?'
>
> Dad thinks about this for a second.
>
> 'About fifty-fifty.'

As he watched this young, beautiful officer traipse past him day after day, John came to a realisation. He'd been right. He *was* meant to be here. What's more, he thought as he caught his uniformed reflection in a nearby window, he looked the part. Six feet tall, fit, a close match for Cary Grant in the right light. He was lanky, sure, but strong for his age. He had striking blue eyes, and he would have a full head of hair for the rest of his natural life, thank god.

'Mate,' Dad says, as if reading my thoughts. 'Just so you know, bald genes travel through the mother's side.'

Dammit. He's right.

2

PURELY ACADEMICAL

John was one of 180 cadets in his class – class 171. Over his first few weeks as a cadet, John got to know several of his teachers. He had two primary instructors. One was ex-highway patrol, and his name was Sergeant Morris. John was struck by, and even once attempted to imitate, Morris' carefully coiffed aspect; hair flicked up like a wave beating down on a bevy of lucky waiting surfers. He's like Guy Smiley, thought John to himself. If Guy Smiley hit the gym more. And were human.

Morris would tell John and his fellow cadets inspirational stories of valour and intrigue designed to get their blood well and truly up; the exact kind of incendiary and inspirational crime narratives to heat the marrow of up-and-coming police officers.

The second instructor was named Sergeant Shipp, who was, by all accounts, off his tree. Idiosyncratic on every level, he lived on the northern beaches of Sydney and was regularly referred to behind his back as 'unusual'. Both of these men taught the theory on how to be a competent officer, and, in John's mind at least, did so very well.

The flipside of being flooded with book-learning was drill work: the ruddy, muddy, shouty underside of academy life.

Marching was meant to teach young, wide-eyed future police officers how to be disciplined and how to work as a group – although more often than not, it just taught them how to suppress a cramp from standing in the same spot for a half-hour in driving rain.

Another thing John learned was how to touch-type, thirty words a minute. This was for police reports, hammered through reams of cheap paper – two sheets with carbon paper in between to make a duplicate. This was not what John had envisioned when he signed up, but nevertheless, he found himself led into the typing room, where banks of worn typewriters stared up at him and his classmates, their knotted mess of keys jutting up like angry, verbose teeth. The man who taught them typing was a beleaguered civil servant, about eighty years old, who was sweet enough, but had taken steps to prevent cheating during touch-typing assessments. What he did, much to John's chagrin, was place a custom-made wooden box over each keyboard, with an opening at the front. He would then prompt John and co. to slide their hands in, type blindly, then remove the boxes and see what freakish avant-garde poetry they'd banged out in lieu of the mock police report they'd been told to type up.

> 'Oh!' I exclaim, excited. 'You survived the pain box.'
> 'Yes,' says my father without missing a beat. 'I am the Kwisatz Haderach.'
> I was twelve when Dad showed me David Lynch's *Dune*, and I don't think Mum ever forgave him.

John noticed something else about these typing classes: there were no women there. All who'd entered the academy were assumed to have an innate typing ability, something which seemed odd to him even then. Those who ran the academy presumably thought women were born with several skills, one of which was to take dictation from men in suits as they swished their brandy and as such, this class is not where John met Christine. We're not quite there yet.

Which is a damn shame, because it's rather a lovely story.

But for now, John was learning to type. He sat there, smugly typing away underneath his unwieldy wooden sheath, enjoying the sight of several of the more gym-prone male cadets, perfectly sculpted arses balanced precariously on their tiny chairs, huge simian hands gingerly navigating the tiny keys, brows furrowed and grunting sporadically. It occurred to John, as his concealed hands deftly breezed from letter to letter, that this must be what it was like to watch gorillas quietly, furiously grapple with Rubik's cubes.

John continued to ruminate over this as he proudly withdrew the sheet of paper from its typewriter prison, before whipping it up to his face and being greeted with the fruit of his effortless touch-typing labours —

Slakhdaksjhbdkjaskjdhkasjhd asjdhkajsh andddhdh haskjdhalhd!2 qwueyamndc,x lwajdela wd salkjwadk laskjd lnkaqwlkjd alkmndlwkj lawjdlkjawd.lkjhaw lwihjed l alwijhd awldhkja nw h awlh walj wa w33 lh
    Awkdeh lwajh iu mn,n cnb,mzn,mn awalkj wakl;jm.,mnw lkj w.,knawlkd jnh,na dlkjw l,mn,mn, nwl;kjla nmd

— at which point he resolved to hide his mistakes. With painstaking care, so as not to attract attention, he very slowly lowered the paper from in front of his face to the desk. Then, with deliberate, casual movements, he folded it in half, and calmly slid it beneath his typewriter.

Success.

He looked up to see if anyone had noticed: a single, burly police officer was staring right at him. John was so absorbed in his small victory that, for a brief moment, all he saw was an actual gorilla, uniform far too small for its bulging frame, hunched over a successfully completed Rubik's cube.

The gorilla waved. John waved. The bell rang.

Training to be a police officer was laid out like this: three months at the academy, then nine months placement at a station, under supervision and working with an array of senior officers. Then, at the start of the second year John would go back to the academy for secondary training, followed by more placement. This period helped cadets figure out where they wanted to end up in the New South Wales Police Force, or whether they wanted to end up there at all. John knew exactly what he wanted: put me somewhere as busy as possible, where the action is.

For John, action was the opposite of the academy. The novel moments were overshadowed by endless hours of marching. He hated marching. Partly because it was pointless busywork, but mostly because he was profoundly bad at it. His body had an innate knack for defying choreography; rhythm, even that as staid as a regimented marching beat, made his hair hurt.

John was so bad at marching in formation that his almost wilful lack of coordination somehow managed to spread like a virus to anyone marching nearby.

Typically, when marching, one lifts the left leg up along with the right arm, then changes sides, and keeps this up in a snappy one-two, regimented fashion. John's primary motor cortex, however, evidently saw this as too 'safe', opting instead to lift the right arm and right leg simultaneously, thereby throwing his balance off with such ferocity that he once careened into a nearby cadet headfirst. It was like a curse. The hours he spent marching at the academy give him all the more reason to buckle down and walk on out of there each day with his head held high. Walk. In a straight line.

With no discernible tempo.

Lack of coordination notwithstanding, he was progressing towards his goal smoothly. He had several roadblocks, however, not least of which was his residence with his brother, Michael, and Michael's friend, Gaz, whose name was Gaz because . . . of course it was.

What was interesting was that Gaz and Michael were basically stoners, which made John's entry into the academy a wee bit sketchy at times. Take, for example, the week before John was accepted. Even in the fast and loose eighties in Sydney law enforcement there was a stringent vetting process before someone was brought into the fold. One night, about 11 p.m. in the middle of the week, John was reading in his bedroom, when what sounded like a battering ram slammed against the front door. Concerned it was someone there to form the beginnings of a house party, he threw down his novel and stepped over a pile of old laundry, making his way out into the hall.

The smell of pot smoke, as well as the smoke itself, pressed into him like a wall of cotton. Instantly, he was contact high. He pushed on into the living room, where Michael and Gaz had poured themselves over the brown corduroy couch. Johnny Carson was wrapping up, and the TV was casting flickering lights on the two, who were giggling but otherwise motionless. The room looked, and smelled, like an armpit.

'You hear that?' John inquired. They waved him off, continuing to laugh at the TV. He rolled his eyes, and stomped down the corridor to the front door, which he flung open, only to be greeted by . . .

'Evening. Are you . . .'

The younger of two very serious looking police officers referred to his notepad.

'John Verhoeven?'

John went from foggy to lucid in a millisecond. He immediately straightened up and launched himself into *you'd-better-enun-ci-ate-every-god-damn-word* mode. He smiled pleasantly, and willed his now indolent mouth into motion.

'How can I help the two of you?'

The two cops eyed John up and down, and, apparently satisfied, continued their preamble. 'We're here,' carried on the younger of the two, 'to conduct your inspection. As you were made aware, an inspection of your living area, in order to evaluate your viability as a candidate for the New South Wales Police Force, has to take place. As this is a surprise inspection, you're probably gathering why we're here now, and not earlier, when you were . . . you know, *ready* for it. May we come in?'

'I . . . Uh . . .'

'Not a request, mate.' The older cop had made his debut. He gave a glimmer of a smile – not a nice one, mind – and they pushed past John.

Past John, and into the pot-addled den where John's brother

and his incapacitated friend lay slumped, cackling insanely as *Gunsmoke* blared from the television. John burst in behind the two policemen who stood, transfixed, by the strung-out tableau. The shag-pile carpet was peppered with spent joints, there were burger wrappers piled on the coffee table, and there was a fug of freshly smoked weed so potent John could feel himself getting higher still just standing there.

After an achingly long pause, the younger cop turned his head slowly towards a nearby closed door, and pointed. From underneath, the faint hum of very strong, very constant LED light oozed out in a steady stream. The older officer walked over, nudged the door with his foot . . . and it creaked open to reveal a small but fertile crop of home-grown marijuana plants. They were covered with buds, and they stood proudly under a bank of jury-rigged lights.

There was a pause so pregnant it could comfortably have borne octuplets. Then, very deliberately, doing everything short of whistling nonchalantly, the older officer pulled the door shut, and he and his partner continued inspecting the house. They disappeared out of sight.

John stood rooted to the spot, and turned his head slowly to look at Michael and Gaz. They were both staring up at him, mouths fantastically agape. A tiny pool of piss began forming between Gaz's legs.

John nervously rounded the corner and entered his room, where the two officers were taking notes and talking between themselves. He decided to be blunt, and honest.

'Hi. Is . . . is anything you saw here, in this house . . . going to be a problem?'

They turned to face him. The older cop spoke.

'Out there? No. No, no problem, there wasn't much there and you're straight, so you're fine. No problem. In here, though . . .'

The officer reached down to the bed, and lifted up the book John had been reading.

'Mate. Fucking *Thorn Birds*?'

3

OH CAPTAIN, MY CAPTAIN

John was a sucker for a mentor. After growing up with a strict, often disapproving father, and after being raised on a diet of novels filled with hard-boiled detectives, strong men with square jaws who busted up drug rings, John began to cobble together a composite sketch of a real-life hero he could admire. He'd grown up with loveable weirdos, though, so he wanted to make sure this mentor was a little off-kilter, too. Just to stop things getting boring.

He planned on chopping and choosing, taking an inspirational quote here, a life lesson there, to create in his mind the perfect role model upon whom he could lean in times of trouble. With Julian he found an offsider, sure, and one who complemented him. But Julian also . . . encouraged him. So while his police career was peppered with fellow units, Julian was one in whose presence he would become . . . well, looser.

The academy was, however, full of people who almost steadfastly refused to complement, or compliment, John. In one particularly gruelling class helmed by Sergeant Sweats, a diminutive, angry man with a shock of ginger hair who resembled a 'roided-up Hobbit, John was learning self-defence. For weeks on end the entire class was taken through the finer points of how to disarm an opponent using a baton, how to escape a stranglehold, and how to attempt to use an adversary's weight and strength against them. On this particular day, Sweats had the cadets doing aikido flips on other, less fortunate recruits. Now in this class, there was an unfathomably beautiful officer-in-training named Sue. Sue used to be an air hostess. Because of her looks, she was objectified beyond belief at every turn, though none of this affected her grades, which were exemplary. She conducted herself with dignity and was highly capable, and Sweats had a crush of biblical proportions on her.

Sweats also happened to hate John, for no reason John could ascertain – although to be fair, Sweats was often in charge of supervising the marching, so all things considered, perhaps his hatred was well-founded. Regardless, Sweats viewed this particular class as something truly delicious: he could achieve either of two desirable goals in one swift stroke. He could emasculate and humiliate John, accusing him of gender discrimination for refusing to flip and pin the object of Sweats' affections. Or, if John did relent and proceed with the brutal but necessary lesson, he would have made John look monstrous in front of his peers. Win-win. Kismet. Pure, uncut douchebaggery, to be sure, but a brilliant plan.

What Sweats hadn't counted on was John calling his bluff. He watched John nodding at Sue from across the mat, bowing, and swiftly flipping her through the air and onto the ground, pinning her successfully. The entire class applauded. And in a mad frenzy at his plans having gone lightly awry, Sweats did the only thing his lizard brain could think of.

He charged across the room, and sent his fist flying into John's face. John hit the floor with a sickening crunch, and everyone gasped, stiffening and staring at Sweats, who stood there, glaring, pale and wide-eyed. John slowly stood, nose bloodied, and before heading back to his spot with the rest of the cadets, he helped Sue to her feet.

Much later, after everybody else had left, John went back to the class to shake hands with Sweats, as a gesture of goodwill. It never even occurred to him to report the man, or complain; he figured that if he could be the bigger man – quite literally, in this case – he could set in place a pattern that would do him credit. Regrettably Sweats told him to 'get fucked', but, oddly, after this a switch flicked on in John's brain: if anyone like Sweats took a run at him during his time at the academy, he would kill them with kindness. Even if they did flatten him for his efforts.

A week or so later, this new attitude of John's had well and truly taken up residence. A guest speaker was in attendance, giving a lecture on dealing with explosives. The speaker, a large man with an even larger moustache, had spent the better part of an hour being sarcastic, flippant and generally unpleasant, so at the end of the lecture John took it upon himself to stand and thank said guest speaker on behalf of the class. The man, worn down by the rigours of trying to inspire people who had no interest in being inspired, smiled warily, shook John's hand, and thanked him with a genuine gleam in his eye. From that point on during his first three months at Redfern Police Academy, John became the unofficial spokesman for all of the cadets in F-Troop and would perform his little thank-you ritual. He took pride in it, and so did everyone else. It was like the police equivalent of that creepy song sung by the von Trapp children on the stairs before they headed off to bed.

Maurice Green was one senior man in particular whom John had to really work at. He was a tall, thoroughly muscular, grizzled sergeant with auburn hair and a matching, prodigious moustache, who was in charge of protocol at state level funerals. White gloves, solemn, slow marches, the whole shebang. Diplomats, heroes, politicians, cops who'd been shot in the line of duty, you name it, he protocoled the hell out of it. Whenever a funeral demanded streets to be shut off and an honour guard, a hand-picked group of very senior police would take point. Sergeant Green took his job seriously, and he towed an air of solemnity about him like a hot, hard fog. Everyone at the academy shat themselves whenever he came within spitting distance. Maurice Green had the demeanour of a three-metre statue tasked with guarding a cursed tomb.

If a mountain fucked a Viking, their offspring would be Maurice Green.

One day John's class was gathered up, bundled into a bus, and driven out to Long Bay Gaol. Maurice greeted the busload of incandescently green police cadets and aggressively corralled them to a training course for target practice with the riot squad. Every prison has a riot squad on the premises, just in case the residents take umbrage with the state of their lodgings in a less than civil manner. And the harder the jail, the harder the squad.

This squad proceeded to perform lightning-quick mock takedowns for the cadets, firing off shots at targets and kicking down doors with such vehemence locksmiths a continent away felt an odd, fervent tingle in their nether regions. Maurice led them, taking part with grim, emotionless gusto. The man was proficient at everything but showing any feeling other than pure, sharpened rage. At one point, he demonstrated how, with two shots from a mini-14 rifle, he could puncture a double-brick wall.

When it came time for the visitors to get involved, any whimper, any flicker of emotion from the cadets was met with bellowing roars from Maurice, delivered with the kind of velocity that could permanently part one's hair. Young officers in the making were shaken to their core by this man. He strode from person to person, dredging up minor character flaws and crafting bespoke, handmade insults hewn from the very finest uncut contempt. He strode around, clutching a baseball bat (presumably from home – police don't typically issue sporting equipment as ordnance), informing the cadets that if while firing live ammunition at their targets they so much as glanced away from their rifle sights in the direction of another student, he'd stove their heads in.

Over the course of that afternoon, his fusillade of insults intensified. Cadets began to listen to what he was saying, even if the volume at which he was saying it was making their hair bleed. John, during his shooting exercises, began firing straighter, reacting faster. Maurice strode up, eyeballed him with what could only be described as apparent white-hot madness, then, after a horrendously long pause, gave him a curt nod of approval, and carried on down the line. John figured 'fuming' was Maurice's resting state.

The half-day of weapons training on the dunes near the jail was coming to a close. The wind was whipping up waves of fine sand, and everyone was assembling to get back onto the bus, shaken but invigorated. Green had got through to them. Why had he threatened to beat them to death with a Louisville slugger if they glanced away during target practice? Because if they did so while under fire, with adrenaline pumping, they might accidentally fire live ammunition into a nearby officer or civilian. Every piece of cruelty was a tool to focus the cadets. One could dwell on the symbolism of all this, given that Maurice Green *was* a tool, but regardless of his demeanour, he'd earned a modicum of quiet, unspoken, trembling respect from the class.

Unspoken, that is, until John slipped into his regular role as unofficial spokesperson. He cleared his throat, stepped right in front of Maurice Green and, eclipsed by the looming monolith before him, he began to talk.

'Sergeant Green, my fellow cadets and I would like to thank you for an incredible day. Your insights have been invaluable, and we've all learned a great deal from you. Thanks for your time and effort, Sergeant, I think I speak for everyone here when I say you scared the hell out of us, but it was worth it. Anyway . . . thanks. Thanks very much. Sir.'

John hadn't really planned this far ahead, so he panicked, and began to clap awkwardly. After a moment, everyone else joined in, relieved at first, then genuinely. And from his current vantage point, John watched as tears began to pool in Maurice's eyes. Maurice's bottom lip trembled almost imperceptibly. He then pumped John's hand, almost breaking his wrist. They headed back onto the bus, and John didn't see Maurice Green again.

That is until fifteen years later, when John and his wife were running a small funeral home on the northern beaches of Sydney. There was a large service for a dead police officer, and as John was finishing a phone call outside the main building, an enormous man with a shock of grey hair and an equally shocking grey moustache approached him. Maurice Green shook John's hand warmly, and they easily talked for a half-hour straight. About Maurice's ex-partner who'd died. About how Maurice regretted that his dead friend hadn't warranted a funeral that required marching, or white gloves. And about how, all those years ago, a skinny, scared young cadet had been the first and only member of the academy to thank him for anything, ever.

Maurice also informed John that he'd once seen him march from across the yard at the academy.

'It was like seeing a fucking puppet get electrocuted, mate.'

4

AUTOPSY-TURVY

John was nearing the end of his initial stint of academy time when he saw his first dead body.

On this particular day, there were ten probationary constables with him. Three of the ten were trained schoolteachers. Fully qualified, they had all finished their degrees but then decided not to teach, and instead joined the police academy. It's unclear what it was about the prospect of teaching that drove them towards seeing dead bodies on a regular basis, but there's probably a link there somewhere.

These ten rookies would spend their three months at the academy in initial training, and then be assigned to North Sydney police station. There they would be assigned a mentor, or a partner. A buddy.

'Oh!' I pipe up, cheerfully. 'Buddy like in a buddy-cop film?'

'Like that,' Dad says, 'but with significantly less Danny Glover. We had a very senior officer who was looking after us, and he was a kind of mentor to us. A father figure.'

'Like Danny Glover.'

'Well, no. Danny Glover wasn't in charge of Mel Gibson, they were partners. You're thinking of their boss.'

'Oh, Douglas Todd?'

Dad looks exasperated. 'No, Douglas Todd was the boss from *Beverly Hills Cop*. Do you want to hear about the dead body or not?'

Their senior officer brought them out the front of the station, and a minibus pulled up, the door springing open. The rookies had no idea where they were going, but after about fifteen minutes, all of them talking excitedly, they pulled up outside the morgue. In Glebe. At the time, this was the largest mortuary in the Southern Hemisphere. Maybe it still is.

There are lots of words used to describe dead bodies. In the police force they called them 'dead 'uns' or 'stiffs'. But when a young, green-as-hell John Verhoeven pulled up in front of the Glebe morgue in a minibus, he didn't know that. He didn't know what to expect. And when this nervous little cluster of rookies headed downstairs, they passed through two huge doors and into a vast, cold, very clean room filled with tables. On every single one was a body, and each body was being worked on, simultaneously. They were in all different stages of post-mortem.

Dad pauses and stares at me.

'Why have you stopped?' I inquire.

'Because you're looking a little blanched, Paul.'

'I'm fine,' I lie.

Dad continues staring. 'Then why has your skin turned grey?'

'I'm fine, Dad, keep going,' I sulk, professionally.

A lot of people believe that if you're murdered or something unspeakable happens to you, you have a post-mortem. This isn't always the case. People all over the world meet foul ends, but because of their age, or what people deem normal circumstances, they go to their graves without anyone knowing they were murdered.

John had seen thrillers, so he thought he knew what happened in morgues. They cover the body, they tag the toe. Some serious but slightly kooky mortician delicately peels back a corner of a sheet so a young police officer might cock a curious eyebrow and make a note in his journal.

But movies lie. And on this bright morning in Glebe Morgue John saw that the bodies weren't covered – they were all naked and exposed. The good ones, anyway. The fresh ones. And that's not taking into consideration the huge fridges, or special rooms called The Murder Rooms. John would learn about those later in his career, first hand.

But at this point, the ten rookies were standing there, huddled around near the entrance, visibly reluctant to stray into this grid of active autopsies. Their senior officer told them in no uncertain terms to get a good look at each one, and they began watching not just the bodies, but also the forensic pathologists working on them. They were very, very clinical, and John went from feeling nauseous to wishing he had that kind of detachment, that kind of composure in the face of such horror, something John realised he admired. These experts started out as GPs who became highly specialised over ten years or more. Some doctors gravitate towards feet, some towards teeth, some towards the heart. Some go straight to the cooler.

The rookies saw all the different stages of post-mortems that morning. By the end of it, it's fair to say John was not in a good way. Later, he figured the intention behind saturating them with so many bodies in one go was to numb them to the reality of it, but because of the way the room was laid out, they got hit in the face with new horrors every time they thought they'd adjusted.

Something did strike him, though. Something he hadn't expected. After the first ten minutes or so being surrounded by the dead, John became acclimatised. Those around him seemed to get sicker, whereas he grew fascinated with the process. He asked more questions, took in as much as he could. He appreciated the precision with which the bodies were cut up and examined. This isn't so bad, he thought. I could do this.

Over the course of this story, you're going to hear what my dad's ex-partner Julian would refer to exuberantly, and with great regularity, as 'some heinous shit'. My dad and Julian were inseparable. Lots of kids have a cool honorary uncle, and he was mine. Julian's soon to appear but at this point, Dad hadn't met him. He was a nineteen-year-old rookie wandering around, befuddled, watching corpses being snipped and prodded and folded in on themselves like meat origami.

John saw fifty bodies that day. The room filled and emptied several times while they were there. It was the size of a tennis court. And the worst thing about the day, the absolute worst, was the sound that had the rookies spinning, startled, every time it echoed around the space. John learned that once after a mortician made the incision on a body, he had to peel back the skin and expose the ribs. And to get through those, they needed huge pliers, which they used to snap through the ribs, one by one. The noise was incredible. And awful.

The second worst thing to happen that day soon followed. It was etched into his mind forever. Each table was fitted with a high-pressure hose. Once they'd finished unpacking the stiff like some huge, slack piece of luggage, they'd clean them out. And one of the morticians told John to look inside. The fumes, a mixture of harsh cleaning fluid and bodily gasses, were making him dizzy, and he peered into the hollowed-out body. For a second, the ribs rising to meet the spine made him think he was in the belly of a Viking ship, looking up at the curved beams above him. And just as he was in this moment, in this other place, they applied a tiny, eager saw to the body's temple and began opening the skull, sending a wet, distant buzzing thrumming through the cavity he was inside. He stood up far too fast, and a minute later he was sick. *Exorcist* sick.

The rest of the morning was a haze. They put the subdued rookies all back into the bus. Driving there it had felt like a Contiki tour, but nobody said a word as they returned. Then they went and had a late lunch. Surprising given the circumstances, but they had to eat something. At the local greasy spoon, John ordered the single worst meal he'd eaten in his life. At first he was convinced the food only tasted bad because of the morning they'd had, but he later returned and sure enough, terrible. Biblically rotten. Everything was either burnt or covered in hair, or both. John told his supervisor how utterly woeful the food was, and was met with a thoughtful nod. A month later, this same supervisor at the station would walk over and contract the place to make all the meals for prisoners. Which these days would be considered a form of corporal punishment.

'So what did you order for lunch? Do you remember?' I ask.

Dad thinks for a second, before looking me dead in

the eye and, matter-of-factly, responding '. . . I think I was inspired by all the autopsies. I think I got the chilli.'

Shell-shocked after their grisly crucible, the rookies somberly reconvened. Their supervisor had seen this before – the first day at the morgue was never a pretty sight. John in particular was struggling; he couldn't get the smell out of his head. He sat there, numb, and began to daydream. He'd spent months in the academy learning from books what it meant to be a police officer, performing exercises, doing drills, and nothing even came close to preparing him for what he'd seen today. He felt as if he was sitting outside himself, watching as he tried not to be overcome by existential dread. Or indigestion.

Then, they were all ferried over to the academy. And things got even stranger.

The academy was like a second home to John now. John and his classmates were sequestered in a room on the third floor, and it was early afternoon. Their teacher, an enormous man with flaring nostrils, paced the room.

'This afternoon,' he announced, 'we're going to be talking about something most of you will never use in the field: working undercover. Working undercover means being able to blend in. You'll need to use various tools at your disposal to hide in clear sight, sometimes for long periods.' He paused, eyed the classroom up and down, cleared his throat, and barked a single word. 'Now!'

There was a flurry of footsteps from outside the door, and in a whirlwind of motion it burst open, and in swung the stoned window cleaner. Several of the cadets stood up, alarmed, before the window cleaner took off his wig, put out his cigarette, and shook hands with the officer. 'And to help you today is a recent graduate who will be talking you through some of the finer points of how to blend in if you're lucky enough to go undercover at some point in your careers. Everyone, this is Julian Carpenter.'

And that is how John Verhoeven met his future partner. Julian.

Enter the loose unit.

5

LEN BEATER

And that was it. John was out of his first instalment of classroom time at the academy, and was off to nine months of placement in an actual station, as a functioning cop. On his last day, though, he was sitting next to the oval at the academy after class, with a handful of classmates. A young woman in shorts and a t-shirt, doing laps, passed by, trying to pretend there weren't people staring at her. John watched without paying close attention, then got up to leave. It wasn't until he got home later that night that he grasped exactly who she was.

The girl from the newspaper ad.

Before he knew it, or before he had time to ruminate any further about the girl, John was stationed at North Sydney. He'd seen bodies on gurneys, he'd done unfathomable quantities of paperwork signed in duplicate, and he'd gotten the lay of the land. And one night, he was on switchboard duty.

If you've never seen or heard of a plug and cord switchboard, the kind John was made to operate, imagine an enormous cabinet swarming with wires, attended to by women in neatly tailored suits, in a spy headquarters during the cold war, hands feverishly plugging and unplugging leads with blinding speed. New constables were typically tasked with taking care of this onerous piece of equipment, and one night, mid-shift, a young woman in plainclothes – blouse, skirt and heels – entered the switchboard room.

She was a plainclothes officer; someone not quite undercover, but charged with roaming the beat in something less likely to arouse ire from the layfolk. The hazards of being a woman *and* a plainclothes officer in the eighties was an increased risk of being harassed, which meant you often flushed out a lot more bad people, even if that did mean your neck was on the line more often. So when Christine – *the woman from the paper*, and the woman who ran past him on his final day – rounded the corner, she was spent. It was close to 10 p.m. John clocked her and did a genuine double take, not believing his luck. It's her, he thought. For a brief moment, she made eye contact with him. He snapped his attention straight back to the switchboard, feigning an urgent and sudden interest in the indecipherable grid of leads and buttons.

After a few moments, he decided to glance back to see if she was still there. She was. Her back was facing him, and she was leaning both hands on a desk. His eyes strayed down; she had slipped off both of her heels, and was using one foot to absent-mindedly rub her calf.

'Dad . . .' I cut in. 'These interviews are for posterity and I don't need a love scene on the record. Keep it clean.'

'She's just rubbing her leg!' my father protests. 'She was tired! Isn't that a nice image? Are you getting how it actually looked? She was . . . you know what? I'll show you.'

I begin to object, but before I can stop him, my father has darted enthusiastically across the room, and is resting his hands against an antique table. He clumsily pushes his shoes off, and begins to rub his calf with his big, stupid foot.

'Dad, this is very upsetting.'

'Do you see? Do you get it now? She was —'

I cut him off. 'I get it, Dad. Put your shoes back on.'

What were the odds of her being there? Well, John didn't actually know any of the cadets who'd been posted to North Sydney with him. No one else from his class ended up there; there were well over a hundred cadets at the academy, and he just so happened to be whisked off with a bunch of strangers. And even if they had ended up at the same station, pretty much all their time was eaten up by the buddy period, during which you got six weeks with one senior officer as partner, and another six weeks with a different partner.

And by the time he'd finishing running the odds of seeing her, she'd gone. Once again, he'd missed his chance. But this isn't the story of how John met Christine.

This is how John met Len Beater.

Len had a bad haircut on a good day. He was a fussy man, Lilliputian in stature, brows always furrowed with stress. His entire life, both past and present, was about traffic. He was ex-highway patrol, and he was a real stickler for details, although evidently the details of his unique aesthetic didn't warrant a second look.

Among the police, highway patrol officers were frequently referred to as 'cockroaches', thanks in no small part to their tendency to suck up every morsel of wrongdoing they could to fulfil quotas. Ever felt like you're being victimised by highway patrol officers? That's because, quite often, you probably are. Imagine, then, John's crestfallen face upon seeing each of his fellow cadets at North Sydney get paired up with some manner of superhuman hero-cop, before he ended up shackled to this finicky Baggins. Len looked just as disappointed as John did, which was enough of a shared interest to make the next six weeks nothing if not functional. At least they had that one thing in common.

Vic, the rugged, Germanic officer in charge of assigning each cadet a buddy, smiled at John and Len, bemused. Vic looked less like a police officer and more like a handsome professor, sans the elbow patches. He was hyper-articulate and extremely well spoken. Freed from the shackles of never-ending shift work that wears down all police officers, Vic only had to come in during the days, specifically to supervise and shepherd the probationary constables. He was, in many ways, a matchmaker, and he apparently saw something in the diminutive Len that he thought might suit John.

Years later, John would find himself catching up for a drink with Vic, who admitted in his cups his painstaking, time-tested method for coupling protégé and mentor, thereby crafting the police officers of the future.

Opening his book of names, shutting his eyes and pointing.

The first true hurdle John needed to vault over was his first night shift paired with Len Beater. John arrived, eager and ready, at the station at 10 p.m. for the shift with his buddy. He checked to make sure he was outfitted properly for this foray onto the streets, and was suddenly very aware of the gun in his holster, the baton on his belt, the police hat perched awkwardly on his head. Handcuffs, notepad; he was kitted out, and felt simultaneously very professional, and like a kid playing dress-ups.

Len wasn't around, so John decided to empty his bladder before settling in for a night trapped in a car. Making a beeline towards the men's toilets, he was almost bowled over by a stocky officer with jet-black hair and dead eyes. 'Bathroom's out of order,' he muttered, barring John's way, looking both somewhat awkward and quietly angry. John was about to protest when someone cleared their throat from across the room. John turned.

Len stood waiting by the door, legs snapped shut, his severely mishandled fringe plastered down like a slick, dour curtain. John eyed the black-haired officer pretending not to guard the toilet door, and decided to shake Len's hand instead. Len nodded, and they headed outside. On this particular shift, another senior officer had been assigned to supervise Len on his mentoring duties, a common practice used to ease people in. The senior man in this case was Dunne, a quiet, cheerful and professional forty-something Glaswegian officer.

Things got off to a shaky start when John made for the driver's seat, before being glared at and told off. 'Trainees sit in the back, Verhoeven. The back,' Len stated blankly, pointing at the back seat, as if John needed directions. John meekly slid into the coveted spot shared by those under arrest, and set his brain to 'observe and learn' mode. And that's what John resolved to do: pay attention. Observe and learn.

It looked like it was going to piss down that night. The patrol car they'd been assigned was a bog-standard white Ford Falcon with police markings on it: automatic, six cylinder, utterly unremarkable. Dunne did the driving, saying little to nothing the entire shift, giving Len more room to school John.

John and Len spent the shift keeping their eyes peeled, engaging in stilted small talk. At around one in the morning, they headed over to a grotty little newsagency in the city to pick up some newspapers – all police used to get free newspapers from Surry Hills, literally hot off the presses, the ink still warm on the pages. It was like heading to a bakery in the wee hours to get freshly baked buns, only significantly less carb-heavy.

John was sitting in the back of the car, next to a stack of papers. Len's well of conversation had run dry, and it had started to drizzle gently outside. John's focus drifted and he watched the rain peppering the windshield.

There's a very real feeling, a heat behind the eyes, that hits you when you're nudging towards being sleep deprived. It renders decision-making sketchy at best, and it makes pretending to like someone you're forced to be babysat by nigh impossible. Sitting quietly, however, was a palatable option, thanks to a radio play unfolding throughout the shift. At irregular intervals, it would provide updates from the station, and tonight, the featured player was a white panel van and its occupants, wanted for a spree of very rough, very aggressive break-and-enters on the North Shore. By the time Len and John were headed back to the station with their papery cargo in tow, the count of homes these crims had violated sat in the early twenties.

It was at this point, while crossing the Harbour Bridge in increasingly dense rain, that a white panel van overtook their car. And as it moved past them, John locked eyes with the driver. For a moment in time, the driver looked back, his eyes suddenly wide and staring right at John. He then very, very slowly turned his head back towards the road. Almost as if he thought a police officer's vision was, much like a Tyrannosaurus Rex's, based on movement.

In an instant, the van burst forward and began to peel away.

Len nodded at Dunne, who swiftly flipped on the siren and slammed his foot into the accelerator. John was pushed back against the seat.

The chase had begun.

The first thing John noticed was the warm creep of adrenaline. Have you ever almost got into a fight, been told to cool off, and sat there fuming? Feeling your animal instincts pace restlessly inside your head as you consider whether or not throwing a tantrum is acceptable behaviour for an adult to indulge in publicly? That's what John felt, unable to reach out and grab the fleeing vehicle, unable to drive, and forced to watch as Len's terrible haircut bobbed back and forth in front of him like a demented sunflower.

Dunne, finally back in his conversational element, began to spit updates into the radio while manoeuvring swiftly from lane to lane, staying a car's length behind the van. Curtains of rain bristled over the windshield. He hammered the wipers, and took a sudden left; the van had pulled away with an incredible burst of speed, and for an instant, two of its wheels gently lifted from the ground, before returning with a wet, oily skid.

Len snatched up the radio again. 'Six-two, urgent.'

'Six-two only?' VKG replied.

'Copy.' And, after a moment of static, the driver of 6-2 replied, over the sounds of a siren on his end. 'Here.'

Dunne continued to propel the car into the night with incredible precision. Len, clutching the radio in his stubby hand, sounded slightly unhinged in his reply. 'Six-two, we are in pursuit of a white Holden panel van. Three occupants. Registration Bravo-Mike-Golf, one three three. Heading in northerly direction along Bradfield Highway, they've taken a sudden turn to the left ... we're now headed towards Kirribilli. Blue Street. Hurry. Over.'

John caught a glimpse of his face in the rear-view. His pupils were, at this point, fully dilated. He sat forward, utterly enraptured. After being cooped up in the academy, and lesson after lesson glued to a desk, at last this was what he'd signed up for. Hell, maybe Len wasn't going to be such a shitty mentor after all.

The two cars were pushing ninety kilometres an hour, through back streets in the now relentless rain. Up to Blues Point Road, left down Blues Point Road, past 2SM, then a dangerous turn right all the way to Waverton, all the while watching the panel van ahead of them sway crazily left and right, like an unhinged metronome, fishtailing, sending streams of water directly into the patrol car's windshield. The wipers swatted back and forth like an overworked limb.

While this was happening, other police cars – who had no idea where this chase was going to end, and it *was* going to end, one way or another – were beginning to coordinate and converge on various key points, with the radio network being used to try to anticipate what was going to happen next.

> 'Oh! Like with pre-cogs!' I offer, helpfully.
> 'No,' replies Dad. 'If you put a radio network in a bath it won't see the future, it'll fucking short out.'

Somewhere, in a VKG radio room in a police station nearby, switches were being flicked to combine the police channels of all the surrounding areas – North Sydney, Neutral Bay, Crows Nest – so that cars from every area could coordinate and zero in on an endpoint. And John noticed that all other radio chatter had stopped. There were no updates from patrol cars, and there was no polite banter. Only Len was talking, and everyone else was listening, or replying with a functional yes or no.

John was in the lead car in a high-speed pursuit. He couldn't believe it! He caught sight of his face in the rear-view again, and was struck by how stupidly excited he looked. His mouth was slightly agape, like he'd just been given a particularly unexpected and extravagant birthday cake. He saw his face, suddenly young again, lit by the candles dancing before him. He pursed his lips and took a deep breath.

We're chasing baddies, he thought to himself, unprofessionally.

His reverie was interrupted when the two cars took a corner, and before them, an unlit park and a swarm of incoming police cars appeared. Easily twenty of them, from all different districts, were pulling up on all sides of this enormous park from myriad directions. And, distracted by the sudden blare of lights and noise, the driver of the van apparently stopped paying attention for a moment. Which was all it took for the van to hit the curb at high speed, buckling the axle, and sending it hurtling skyward.

Dunne applied the brakes. John was flung forward; all air in his lungs expelled from his body into the cabin of the car.

The candles, and the cake they adorned, detonated.

6

THE PARK

With a sickening crunch, the white van landed, and began to roll slowly down towards the trees. Dunne took a moment to recover, shaking the dust from his eyes. And as the three of them watched, all still winded from the sudden evasive driving Dunne had managed to pull off, they saw the doors of the van fly open, almost in unison, and three occupants jump out of the still moving, and barely intact, vehicle. They then proceeded to run.

John barely had time to process any of this. He knew that the end goal of any car chase was to force your adversary, for lack of a better word, into a state of recklessness which would get them to crash. Len had done that, with aplomb. But John had never been in a car chase, and had a thick diagonal welt across his torso from where the seatbelt had struck him, and before he could ask Len what to do next, Len did the unthinkable.

Dunne had already burst from the car and had begun chasing one of the men down a side street. Upon seeing this, Len began muttering angrily, swiftly drew his gun, elbowed open his door and bolted after the men.

Which was problematic, John noted, because all three suspects had broken off and run in different directions. He watched as Len, gun drawn, legs pumping furiously, sprinted after the one who'd disappeared into the blackness of the park. John undid his belt, winced, and looked around, dismayed; none of the other police cars were close enough to give pursuit, instead cordoning off the surrounding area to stop any traffic getting in. He opened his door, climbed out, and there, across from him and trying to sneak away using parked cars as cover, was the man he'd made eye contact with, wearing a faded Countdown t-shirt.

John ran at him.

He didn't draw his gun, mind you. It's important to note that nothing had been mentioned about these men being armed, so Len pulling his weapon and running off, unaccompanied and in the dark, leaving behind his trainee partner, was bizarre behaviour. John registered how easy it would be to end this chase if he simply brandished his firearm at the fleeing figure, but opted not to act like a complete dick, and instead sped up.

He'd almost caught the man when two shots rang out from the park.

John skidded to a halt and turned, leaving the man to continue into the night. Shots fired. This was not good. This was very, extremely not good. Was John responsible? Should he have gone into the park with Len Beater? Should he have drawn his gun and run headfirst into the darkness with all the forethought and sagacity of a runaway train?

Hell, thought John, packing it in and running back towards the park. What if they *were* armed? The rain picked up. John was wet through, and could barely see as far as the other cars any more. He made it back to the police car, hoping Dunne had returned.

He hadn't. So despite his shaking hands, John steeled himself and got on the radio. And on his very first night on patrol, having literally never once used a police radio before, spoke the following words:

'Shots fired.'

In the eighties in Sydney, hearing those words over the radio was a truly rare event. Not only that, but as John went on to explain to VKG, his hands shaking, his partner was missing. And when asked where Len had gone, John understood he couldn't provide anything approaching a satisfactory answer; he'd been so wrapped up in his head during the chase that he honestly couldn't say which park they were at. And John not knowing the name of the park after saying 'shots fired' was a bit like running into parliament, and, after yelling 'He's got a gun' and being asked 'Who?' replying, '. . . Oh, I don't know, someone. Sorry, I wasn't paying attention.'

Upon these words being uttered, Pol-Air, the dog squad, all detectives, *everyone* was mobilised, and the Sydney-wide police radio network was switched to John's car, gazing at it with the singular focus of the Eye of Sauron. To the tiny plastic box in his trembling hand. Dozens of police that night, across a multitude of departments, would have heard him stammering away, explaining with as much dignity as he could muster that Len Beater 'wasn't there' and that 'the situation was normal'. He understood after a moment that he was, without meaning to, imitating Han Solo as he tried to pass himself off as a stormtrooper on the Death Star, before firing his blaster into the radio. John wondered if he could get away with a similar stunt. He figured wrapping up the conversation by unloading his gun into the receiver wouldn't go down *super* well, so he stayed his hand.

At this point, all over the city, the radio scanners of tow-truck drivers flared to life, awakening the great steel beasts much the same way that the smell of impending decay rouses a buzzard. Back then, towing was a first-in, best-dressed industry: drivers waited by radios, waiting for police chatter about crashes, then headed there as fast as they could to stake a claim on the leftovers. It was predatory and exploitative, and, coupled with the fact that news media were tuned in to the same scanners, meant that crash sites got very crowded in a matter of minutes.

A dense mob of onlookers formed, held back by police, and John stood there, panicking, sodden, face pelted with torrents of rain, thinking that Len had been shot. Sirens blared from every direction.

And just as John was about to get back on the blower and mumble another indistinct plea for help, Len emerged from the darkness of the park. His gun was, John noticed, thoroughly holstered. 'You all right?' John ventured, unsure how to ask whether or not Len had just shot a man.

As if reading his mind, Len, in a deadpan voice and without breaking his gait, replied, 'I missed. Lost him. Don't . . .' At this point he made eye contact with John, and as if each word was underlined, spoke more emphatically than before. 'Don't bother reporting this. I'll handle it.'

By which Len meant: 'don't report that a senior officer lost his shit, caused a crash, then chased and shot at an unarmed man, with witnesses within earshot. Don't report shots fired.'

Shots fired.

Shit. Shit shit shit.

'What's the problem?' asked Len.

John realised he'd been swearing out loud.

'Uh . . . Well, after I heard the shots, I assumed the worst. I called it in.'

'You didn't say shots fired.'

'I did.'

There was a long pause. A big vein above Len's left eye pulsed angrily, and the corner of his mouth puckered. His bowl-cut fringe clung to his forehead, plastered down with a mixture of rain and sweat, and finally, it dawned on John who Len reminded him of: Grandpa Munster. I shouldn't laugh, John thought to himself. Grandpa Munster wasn't prone to shooting people in the back.

Len, having processed the situation, finally replied. 'Shit. Shit shit shit.'

In the eighties, each bullet supplied to individual officers was inventoried and accounted for. They were called Police Specials, and they were custom-made for the New South Wales Police Force. They had a specific purpose: to enter the body, but not go through it. They were designed to go in two inches, and then break apart, effectively eviscerating internal organs.

'Hang on, hang on,' I chime in. 'I know this is going to come up, and I'm not judging you or anything, obviously. But why the hell do cops need to damage the human body like that? Isn't that a tad excessive?'

'Think about it, mate,' says Dad. 'You don't want a bullet passing through the person you're firing at, and hitting a bystander, do you? I mean, think about *Dirty Harry*. Don't think about Clint, who talks to empty chairs nowadays. Think about *the* Dirty Harry, aiming his .44 Magnum at a child rapist. Now in reality, if he fired that gun and there were fifteen people in a line behind him that bullet would pass clean through every one of them. A thin wall of skin and bone doesn't do shit to stop a projectile travelling at three and a half thousand feet per second.'

Hearing Dad speak so matter-of-factly about rupturing organs and explosive ordnance makes me feel odd, as if I've walked in on him doing something possibly untoward. Maybe it's practised, maybe he's just trying to impress me. Hell, maybe it's a bit of both.

What those two missing bullets would mean was an ocean of paperwork. It could've been dealt with on the QT, sure, but not now that John had sounded off to every single law enforcement agency in Sydney. Len glared into the middle distance. There were police cars and media from arsehole to breakfast. Every one of the van's occupants was in the wind, and both Len and John began taking notes and wrapping up. It would take some time to disperse the crowd, and there were reports to be made, witnesses to take statements from and other housekeeping to get done, none of which was made easier by the ungodly hour and the unrelenting rain.

Fifteen minutes later, the crowd had yet to dissipate, and Len was on the radio, nodding and muttering. Dunne had returned empty-handed, and was taking statements across the park. John had decided to stand back under an awning, assuming (correctly) that Len was in no mood for company at the present time. He scanned the crowd. How many of them had heard the shots? How many of them had seen the crash? His mind drifted as he panned across their faces.

Which is when he saw a man behind the throng of looky-loos, perched on a shitbox Honda 125. A man wearing a Countdown t-shirt. A man who took a moment too long to register John. For John, you see, was hopped up on adrenaline, and had already cleared the line of people before the burglar could start up the bike. And as he fumbled at the ignition, John, sprinting at full speed, left the ground with all the velocity of a cannonball. John, gangly, eyes wide, face frozen in a manic grin, legs pulled up to his chest, uniform plastered to his body, hung in the air for a second, before extending both legs. His feet crashed with a sickening thud into the chest of the man, who popped cleanly out of his seat like a champagne cork exploding from the bottle.

John's momentum carried him over the bike and sent him tumbling end over end. He landed badly before scrambling up and pinning the man down. He then blinked the rain out of his eyes, cleared his throat, and performed his very first arrest.

In the rain, with a crowd of people watching agog, he pulled out his handcuffs and began to put them on the man. John had, however, forgotten how to apply them properly. He fumbled for a while. The afterglow of a superb martial arts manoeuvre was beginning to wear off, and onlookers began to giggle. Several were muttering how *they* would put the handcuffs on, John realising he was within earshot of what were effectively backseat-arresters.

Keen to get the whole sordid affair over and done with, the man in the Countdown shirt twisted his head back, eyeballed John, and muttered, 'Just whack the fucking things on. You have to . . .'

John replied impatiently, trying to keep his voice down to save some face, 'I am, I'm . . .'

They argued back and forth as John struggled valiantly.

Finally, the man beneath him sighed and cut him off. 'Have you ever done this before?'

John paused, and went red. He continued impotently fumbling with the stubborn cuffs. 'Yes.'

'How many times?'

A pause. 'Heaps.'

'Heaps?'

'Yes.'

Finally, a click. John gave a shudder of relief; the kind you get after you hang a piss you've been holding in the entire day.

Len looked up, radio in hand, to see John finally getting the cuffs on. He looked at the man, looked back at John, processed what he was seeing, and with the faintest hint of a smile on his face, turned back to the radio.

'This is car 6-1. Suspect in custody. Over.'

7

OFF THE CUFF

A brief aside on the nuances of cuffing a suspect.

In theory, you need to hold both cuffs, and then whack them wristward, whereupon the cuffs part like slick metallic gates, before ratcheting shut with a satisfying series of clicks.

In practice, in the rain, a fatigued and anxious young officer might neglect to hold down the small button on each cuff. Without pressing these buttons down, the metal cuffs won't retract. They will instead smash into the suspect's wrists, causing said suspect to react very physically, perhaps prompting them to shake free of the flimsy hold you have them in. Maybe they'd call you a bad name as they mule-kicked you and fled into the night.

John did, as we've established, manage to get the cuffs on without anything nasty going down. But then what? He had an enormous man, conspicuously bigger and stronger than himself, soaking wet, face-down on the footpath with his arms cuffed behind his back. John's knee was nestled against the man's spine, and his hands stung from repeatedly slamming the cuffs downwards. Drowsy onlookers watched, appraising him with narrowed, condescending eyes. Ever seen a mother or father with a loudly crying child on public transport, suffering an onslaught of withering looks from judgemental bystanders who've never had, and will never have, kids? That's the look.

Now, John had to get the man to his feet. This proved tricky. The man had no way of standing without assistance, and, given his bulk, what commenced was a full three minutes of two men swearing at each other and becoming hysterical; every time John managed to precariously get Countdown to his feet, the handcuffed man would slip and crash down again.

John would then apologise, Countdown would mutter impatiently that they were doing it wrong, and they'd try again. Eventually they came up with a system: John would use the man's restrained arms as a handle, yanking them back and pulling upwards, and Countdown would strain in the opposite direction, with both men chanting in unison, 'Push! Push! Push!' It was like a grimy, makeshift Lamaze class at two in the morning. Eventually, after a lot of pushing, the 76-kilo officer managed to somehow negotiate the 110-kilo criminal to his feet. It's a boy, John thought.

Once this miracle was accomplished, what passed between the two was a bizarre kind of admiration. They'd run this harrowing gauntlet together. They had an accord.

This reverie of fellowship forged through a shared trauma lasted right up until the moment John forgot to hold down Countdown's head as he put him into the back of the wagon, where he whacked it with some force on the top of the door. Shaken from his state of delirious chumminess, the man resorted to sulking instead.

And that was how John made his very first arrest.

John had expected to carry on with this case but Countdown was soon ferried over to the detectives' office where he was interrogated well into the morning hours. John spent a while dwelling on how he should be the one doing the interrogation, but eventually accepted that's just how it was. He was junior, and the glory went to those higher up. After a moment he cottoned on to the fact that he still hadn't taken a slash all night, and headed into the now unimpeded bathroom. Sitting there, eyes burning from exhaustion, he gazed at the back of the toilet cubicle door. About halfway up, clear as day, was a striking maroon lipstick impression, like a stamp on the filthy wood.

John thought back to earlier, recalling the intensity with which the officer with the black hair had insisted he not enter the bathroom. Clearly this stall was the scene of . . . well, not a crime, but something that in all likelihood would be clearer if he brought a blacklight in and gave the place a sweep. Feeling suddenly unwell at that prospect, John finished up and headed back to see out the shift.

And see it out the three of them did. John, Len and Dunne spent what remained of the evening driving around, gently recovering from their misadventures, with Len coming over oddly chatty. John found this sudden talkative streak some kind of overcompensation on Len's part. In the same way that when a sibling thumps their head, and before their brain can register the pain and indignity, you try to throw them off-balance with distracting banter, perhaps Len figured he could divert attention from the shots fired incident.

By the time they'd got back to the station soon to clock off, Len's annoyance at the situation had turned inwards. John was typing up a report and Len checked it, nodding quietly. 'Yeah. I . . . shouldn't have done that,' he said, with an air of contrition, before returning to his own report.

The arrest had by now been handballed up the chain of command. Due to the fact that this crew had robbed so many places, it was deemed above Len and John's pay grade. So as much as John wanted to show initiative and chase leads, he was, for now, powerless as the case got carried away from him, borne aloft like the precious purloined cargo of stoic ants at a picnic. Len told John this was par for the course, adjusted his phenomenally shitty hair, and poured himself another acrid coffee. He offered John the same. Out of politeness, John took a cup and forced it down.

John watched the flurry of activity around him, and understood that Len was right: 'par for the course'. And as the reality of the situation dawned on him, a little bit of his excitement drained away. Spirited away by the detectives – aka the 'glory boys' – a case John felt ownership over was being shared around like tips at the end of the night. It didn't matter that he'd been given the hundred; now everyone got a piece. But he was, when it came right down to it, a probationary constable. He was a mote of dust caught on an eddy, barely noticed in the storm now making its way up the command chain.

After they'd returned to the station, he'd chatted with Dunne, congratulating him on his exemplary driving, instinctively slipping back into his hyper-polite, von-Trapp-of-the-class persona. Dunne, John discovered, had been an officer of some renown in Scotland. He was tall, broad-shouldered, had prematurely greying temples and hands the size of baseball mitts. He had a perpetually even temper, rarely getting excited about anything at all, which he claimed made him perfect for driving in high-speed pursuits.

'Listen, mate,' chuckled Dunne, his thick accent rendering his words almost indecipherable at this early hour. 'Don't go using words like "exemplary". This isn't a written exam. If you don't figure out how to talk like everyone else you're going to have a fuck of a time getting people to like you. So don't use big words.' He paused, and not unkindly added, 'And don't call "shots fired" on your buddy. Come to me next time, I'll do it. He can't get mad at me. He thinks I'll beat him senseless. Once heard him refer to me as a "brick shithouse".' He patted John on the shoulder, and turned to leave. Then he paused and turned back, grinning. 'Good job, though. I saw that tackle. Not seen a beanpole move like that before.'

John tapped absent-mindedly at the keys of his typewriter. He liked Dunne.

And he felt a certain *something* after their talk. He didn't feel like a hero exactly. He did, however, feel a creeping sense of pride in his work. On his first night out on patrol, he'd been in a car chase, tackled a suspect and handcuffed someone for the first time, albeit clumsily. He'd also called in 'shots fired', something most officers never got to do, and despite the chaos this caused, he felt a little chuffed at having made an impact on the contours of the evening. What's more, he'd managed to get his buddy, Len Beater, to warm to him.

Well, perhaps warm was a slight exaggeration. Lukewarm. Tepid. Old bathwater perhaps, but things certainly weren't frosty any more.

'Up. Up up up. You're in my seat.'

Len was looming, or attempting to loom, over John, tired eyes as small as belt holes. 'Get up.'

John sprang to his feet, mumbling an apology, and made his way outside for a breath of fresh air.

It was frosty out there, too.

8

ROUTINE BUSINESS

After such a brazen opening night, the show that was John's induction into station life slipped into monotony fairly quickly. Not that he wasn't over the moon to be away from the academy, but he did receive a crash course in the drudgery of everyday station work. The bread and butter of being a station constable consisted of the following:

- Answering the phones
- Fingerprinting each prisoner who was brought in and charged
- Photographing said prisoners with a powerfully shitty camera, jammed onto a flimsy aluminium rod
- Filling out prisoners' paperwork, aided by stamps the size of coffee mugs and pens always on the verge of running dry

John had the most trouble with fingerprinting. First, under the watchful glare of the soon-to-be-incarcerated suspect, he'd have to squirt a decidedly fecal deposit of ink onto the inkpad, then massage it in. The pad would thank him for his troubles by, in front of everyone, making a wet, squelchy farting sound. Which didn't lessen John's perpetual discomfort in holding the hands of strangers, then rolling their fingers across an inky pillow under the harsh pharmacy-grade lighting.

Most people being fingerprinted were drink-drivers – confused, scared and disoriented – hauled in unceremoniously and often looking like wounded puppy dogs. Every time he saw their big, shiny eyes, John would briefly consider apologising for being so intrusive. Then the farting sound would fill the room, and he'd promptly hurry through the rest of the procedure.

John soon understood, though, that as much as they might hate it, 90 per cent of people being fingerprinted were thoroughly compliant because they knew they were fucked. The architecture of the dock where these procedures took place – photographs, fingerprints, vital information such as hair colour, eye colour, height, weight, distinguishing marks – seemed innocuous, but it filled people with the sense that they were now well and truly on the grid. Mundane information can feel more personal than big, grandiose revelations; making someone lift their shirt at 3 a.m. to show you their birthmarks as they slowly coat themselves with a sheen of shame-induced panic-sweat was a hugely confronting experience for many new officers.

If, after this gauntlet, bail was refused, John then had to carry out another of his menial tasks: taking the prisoner out to the cells. The cellblock itself was 130 years old, and in mid-winter, without heating, the cells were freezing. Steel doors with plates that dropped down, bolts a foot long that slid into place; the entire thing was deliberately demoralising, which proved useful when the perp was hardened, and damaging if the perp was a young, confused drink-driver whose parents weren't answering the phone.

These cells weren't allowed to house women, incidentally. If one was arrested, they'd then have to be conveyed over to Central. Going there was like stepping back in time two hundred years. It was, as John would later refer to it, feudal. A dense, impenetrable, bombproof ant hill where many of the major crimes in Sydney were worked on – and, as John soon discovered, quite a few were perpetrated.

But John wasn't at Central. He was still a rookie, pulling the night shift at North Sydney. And the thing about night shifts is that your circadian rhythms, at around two or three in the morning, get, in the words of John's colleagues, 'fucked, mate'.

In wintertime, in the mornings, John would leave the station after a night shift, and head to his beautiful new Volkswagen. Not long after he started at the station he'd needed a new car, and had made the mistake of idly browsing way out of his price range. The VW in question was pristine. It was the 13 millionth VW manufactured in the world, and had a plaque on it to indicate that fact. He'd seen it for sale at a small motor show, and mentioned it to Len, who became oddly paternal and offered to have a word with the owner to help get the sale over the line. So, in full uniform, John and Len hopped in a police car and headed up the highway. John stayed in the car and watched as Len chatted with the owner. He took note of the body language: a knowing nod here, and pat on the arm there. He couldn't hear what they were saying, but when Len walked back over and threw him his own clumsy take on what could kindly be called a wink, John knew the car was his.

So a week after getting this car, this gorgeous white Volkswagen emblazoned with a plaque and cleaned to within an inch of its life, John staggered from the station at the end of another night shift and hopped in. After making it to a set of lights near the

Harbour Bridge, he came to a stop, and while waiting for the lights to change, promptly fell asleep. An impatient beep from behind shocked him back awake, and he fumbled, driving far too fast for a moment before steadying himself and returning to his normal drive home. 'Shit. OK. You're OK,' he muttered to himself, calm in the knowledge that the adrenaline now coursing through his body would get him home. He breathed easy, and came to the next set of red lights.

Another honk. He screamed and woke up. Again. He'd fallen asleep, again.

This continued all the way home. Red light. Honk. Scream. Muttering. Driving. Stopping. Red light. Honk. Scream. Muttering. Driving. Stopping. Then, finally, he pulled into his garage, slapped himself a few times in the face, stripped off, collapsed into bed . . . and lay there, eyes lasered open, brain awash with an endless stream of thoughts, utterly unable to sleep.

9

GET IN, LOSER. WE'RE GOING SHOPPING.

After a week or so of being the third wheel, jammed in the back of the Falcon like a guest of Dunne and Beater, John was informed that it was *his* turn to drive. He was incredibly nervous. The bar had been set extremely high by Dunne, who drove with almost mechanical speed and precision. And to make matters worse, over the past week, John had learned that Beater had all the good humour on the roads of a freshly divorced driving instructor.

Not that this was a bad thing. At least, not so far as the reputation of the New South Wales Police Force was concerned. The moment you put on the uniform and hit the streets, you were on show. If John drove like an arsehole straight out of the gate, he'd not just make Len look bad, he'd make the whole force look bad. And Len had, if nothing else, a strong sense of pride about the force.

So when Len and John pulled away from the station, and halfway down Miller Street during the lunch rush Len asked John to reverse park into a space so tight it could compress coal into a diamond, John baulked. Internally. He didn't say anything, because he'd already told Len he was quite the driver, and here they were, doing a little driving test of their own. With hundreds of bystanders.

People were sitting on benches, eating their lunches, watching with idle curiosity as John, sweating police specials, turned on his indicator.

'Paul . . . Would it be funnier, or more interesting . . . if I pranged the car?'

I stare at Dad, eyebrows raised.

'Dad. You can't pick what is and isn't funny and lie about it to make the story work. Either you did bang into something or you didn't. It . . . wait. Have you been bullshitting me to make this story shinier?'

Dad is immediately offended. 'No! I'm asking if I should . . . I'm asking from a comedic standpoint, would crashing the car be funnier?'

'Yes. Yes, obviously,' I reply. 'And you know that or you wouldn't have asked.'

My blood is up. We sit there in silence.

'Well, I did.'

One look at him tells me this is true. Dad only has one tell, in that he has none. His face gives everything away the moment he opens his mouth.

Honest to a fault.

A man drinking from a thermos started and burned his crotch as John, squinting, straining, sweating, hit a bollard with the rear fender of the patrol car. He didn't dare look over at Len, whom he could hear breathing hard through his nose. He knew the face he'd see when he did turn to his left: mouth pursed, brow furrowed, blond hair clinging to the forehead like the dog-eared pages of a well-read book. He wrestled with the wheel, quickly pulled away from the bollard, mouthed the word 'sorry' at the alarmed businessman with the freshly scorched dick, and, somehow, finished the reverse park without any further incident.

I chuckle.

Dad throws me a look, and I know exactly what he's thinking: *Shut up, dickhead, you don't even drive.* He's right. I still cannot drive. I give him a look in return, and nod an apology.

'Did you report it?' I ask.

'Of course. Everything has to be noted down. But after a while those little corners you tuck in neatly get a little ragged, it happens. Just a little. At this point, though . . . boy scout.'

Len was, when it came down to it, a traffic cop. There was no shame in this. Back in those days, John would attend about ten motor vehicle accidents per shift, as would every other car in the area. In the eighties, cops had to attend every tin-pot accident, and for John that meant being scrutinised by someone who took traffic infractions very seriously (Len was bordering on a hobbyist when it came to the minutiae of traffic infractions). This meant that his first week after the chase consisted primarily of Len tutting with almost metronomic regularity as John fumbled his way from accident to accident.

Near the end of the week, in the middle of a shift, Len and John were near Mosman, idling in the car park of a certain middling burger chain. John had ordered his favourite – a fish burger, large fries, and a strawberry shake – when a call came in about an accident. Len threw his food into the bag, hurled it over his shoulder on to the back seat, and bellowed, 'GO! SIREN! GO!'

John, startled, dropped his burger and hit the accelerator. As they hurtled out into traffic, the momentum sent the contents of John's enormous cup up towards its flimsy lid, which protested for a millisecond, bulging outwards, then popped clean off, sending frothy pink muck flying in all directions.

John, to his credit, didn't swerve about idiotically; he just sat there and copped it, with a look of dignified exhaustion on his face. Len copped the brunt of the blast and was covered in shake and fries, giving him the appearance of someone who'd received a fatty tarring and feathering.

The rest of the shift, made up mostly of minor traffic infractions, was completed caked in strawberry shake. By the time it dried and hardened, the car stank of it. Len made John stay back after his shift to clean it, and as John scrubbed and pulled a hunk of crumbed fish out from under a sodden seat, he conceded he was probably in the wrong this time. He resolved to never again order a strawberry shake while in uniform.

Over the following weeks, Len gradually filled John in on his core ideology. You see, Len was obsessed with statistics. And after years as a cop obsessed with traffic infractions and car accidents, he'd come up with a theory: old people were the problem. Instructors at the academy had drummed into John the old adage that the youth were the scourge of the roads, and that they needed to be watched carefully and penalised harshly for any vehicular misdeeds. Len, though – Len had it in for the olds. One slow afternoon, he seized John and led him to a filing cabinet. He opened it, rifled around, and pulled out a folder bursting with incident reports, hundreds of them.

He laid the folder on his desk.

'Right. There's a hundred traffic accidents here. Some bad,

some very bad, some just prangs, but . . . Sit down, and we'll start pulling out one at a time. At random. You'll see.'

John, sceptical, pulled out a report. Three cars rear-ended, two taken to the hospital. Caused by a driver not looking where they were going. And the perpetrator was . . .

'Sixty-eight. Sixty-eight years old. Huh.'

Len nodded and gestured towards the folder. 'Another one.'

John flipped through and grabbed another from the pile.

'Pedestrian struck by a car at a set of lights, dead on arrival. Driver taken into custody . . . Shit. Seventy-two.'

Len unconsciously rubbed his hands together – there's always something energising about having a pet theory vindicated – and gestured again at the folder.

They sat there for a half-hour, compiling the average ages of those who caused traffic accidents, and found that most offenders were over fifty, and the worst were past their late sixties. This, Len pointed out, was why he took what he referred to as a 'special interest' in booking older drivers for minor infractions; drivers often conflated respect for the elderly with giving them a pass when it came to their behaviour on the roads.

But it never sat particularly well with John that over the weeks they spent as buddies, he saw Len regularly pull over older drivers – drivers who'd done nothing so far as he could tell – take their details down, then head back to the station gleefully to have their licences revoked on technicalities. Len called it 'preventative', but the idea of a doddering old grandma being unable to fishtail her way to the pharmacy for much-needed medicine didn't sit right with John. It brewed a nauseating mixture of approval and harsh disapproval in John's mind that wouldn't dissipate. And it began to make John feel even more ambivalent about Len.

At least, until they were on patrol one day, heading down the highway, and a sedan driven by a man in his eighties pulled out into oncoming traffic without so much as a glance at the road. Several cars swerved violently to avoid him, and Len promptly flipped on the siren. Moments later, he was standing over the man, who looked scared and disoriented. Len was blunt, and the man could see there was no arguing.

If there was one thing John liked about Len at this stage in his career, it was this: There was no grey with Len.

But there soon would be.

10

BROKEN TOWS

As John had learned from Len, tow-truck drivers in Sydney at this time were almost predatory. Rather than settling into a neat symbiosis where they cleaned up the city, grooming it like birds pecking ticks from the back of a surly rhino, they were vultures. And as Len pointed out, they were quite often run by bikie gangs, or the mafia. It was, as Len often said, a bit of a clusterfuck.

One morning John and Len got a call to attend an accident in Cremorne. As they pulled up, John saw a young woman surrounded by four tow-truck drivers, trucks parked nearby, their body language mirroring that of slavering hyenas closing in on their prey. The woman was clearly distressed.

Each driver desperately wanted the tow for themselves. Certain panel beaters were keen for the drivers to tow ruined, wrecked, dented cars to them to get worked on, and would pay a thousand dollars per car, cash in hand. The owner of the ruined car typically couldn't (or wouldn't) negotiate with an enormous, frightening bastard, and if the car couldn't be driven, it had to be towed.

The woman, standing out the front of a service station, near her incapacitated sedan, was being told this by four of the largest men John had ever seen. They were inked to the hilt.

'Paul. You know how sharks have those black, dead eyes?'
'Yeah,' I reply.
'Well,' continues Dad, 'they didn't have those. They were human.'

And they were telling this poor young woman that her car had to be towed. Couldn't she see how utterly wrecked it was? the drivers asked, looming over her. Len gave John a nod and, while he adored this kind of job, told him to 'handle it'. He wanted to see if John had learned anything during their time together.

John surveyed the scene. Over by the service station was the woman's car, a green sedan, slightly crumpled at the front. She'd clipped some kind of bollard, which had remained pretty much undamaged. Nearby was the woman, hemmed in by the quartet of gas-bagging morons. The tow trucks were parked across the street. Even empty, they looked predatory.

His eyes scanned back over the car. The damage really wasn't that bad, certainly not dire enough to warrant it being towed. The wheel arch had been largely buckled inwards and was pressing into the tyre, which was on the verge of bursting from the pressure. There were some scrapes running along the side, too, but nothing severe. But the drivers did have a point; this car couldn't technically be driven anywhere.

At this point, John was startled out of his investigative reverie by the sound of raised voices.

And that's when he made his decision.

He walked purposefully over to the garage and headed inside. The drivers stopped yelling and watched, curious. Their curiosity turned to something else when John emerged moments later, the whites of his eyes visible all the way around each iris, clutching an enormous iron rebar. He began to walk towards them.

John walked past them and made for the car. Bending down, he put the rebar beneath the arch, and with all the strength he could muster, began prying upwards. Next to four men practically hewn from pure muscle, this gangly rookie cop straining at an iron bar almost the length of his body must have looked ludicrous. John realised that if he pulled too hard and slipped, the bar might puncture the wheel. He felt metal grinding and shifting under his grip. He shut his eyes, and . . .

Clunk. The arch sprang back into shape, and the wheel made a rubbery *flump* noise. He cautiously opened one eye, his entire body braced to give an apology . . . But evidently, he'd somehow pulled it off. The arch was still wrecked, but it was back where it belonged, and, more importantly, so was the wheel. And it wasn't punctured. The car was, more or less, driveable. Mission accomplished.

He turned slowly towards the tow-truck drivers and their prey, held his arm out, and let go of the bar ninety degrees from his body. It dropped like a mic, and hit the ground loudly.

And that was that. The drivers skulked back to their vehicles and glared at John and Len in a way that indicated they wouldn't forget this; Len later told John they genuinely wanted to inflict some bodily harm that day. John had yanked a payday out from under them. The woman thanked John profusely, and explained that they were trying to charge thousands, insisting the car absolutely had to be towed. He learned that the service station attendant was the one who'd called the police, when he saw four large men getting verbally aggressive with a young woman. After he'd taken a statement and the woman had driven her now functional car away, John made a point of thanking the attendant.

As he sauntered back to the car, Len looked him in the eye and nodded.

'Way to bar up, John.'

John's eyes widened. Not only had Len just made a joke . . . but a dick joke. John smiled to himself on the way back. Maybe he had found a decent mentor after all.

Later that afternoon, John relayed the day's events to Dunne, who, after rolling his eyes, set him straight. Apparently, Len had never buddied up with anyone before. Apparently, Len had serious issues with confrontation – most of the time. And apparently, Len was only good at traffic and statistics, and tended to fold up uselessly whenever confronted by actual, dicey day-to-day police work.

John understood, crestfallen, that Len hadn't sagely observed his young rookie partner handle a situation involving potential bodily harm, coiled and ready to step in at a moment's notice.

He'd hidden behind a fucking newspaper.

11

TAKING STOCK

After his impromptu repair stunt, John found himself filled with a sort of newfound confidence. It's not that he felt he was slipping towards breaking or bending rules and regulations, it's that he felt a little more . . . resourceful. Adaptable. Just a little. And after another three weeks, Len approached John one morning before the shift started and shook his hand awkwardly. 'That's it,' he said. 'End of our buddy period. Nice working with you,' all with barely a hint of emotion in his voice.

John briefly considered giving Len one of his thank-you speeches, the kind he used to be so fond of. But he felt he now knew what kind of man Len was. He was a man who rarely took action, which explained how badly things went when he *did*, a man more comfortable handing out tickets than doing what many cops would deem 'actual' police work.

John became aware he'd been running through this character assessment in his head as he continued to shake, staring right into Len's eyes. For a full twenty seconds he shook Len's hand, nodding in agreement at the profundity of his own powers of perception.

Len yanked his hand back, and, using that same hand, reached up and gingerly patted John on the arm.

'Good work, mate.'

And with that, he walked off.

The station was more crowded than normal that day. The rookies who'd come from the academy with him were buzzing about, and many were congregating around a board on the wall, which was peppered with sheets of paper.

'New buddy day, buddy boy.' Dunne was standing behind him. He clapped a hand down on John's shoulder, and exhaled loudly.

'Who'd I get? Not another Len. Please . . . Not another Len.'

Dunne chuckled. 'Nah, mate. You got Woodstock. Oh! There he is now.'

Dunne's enormous arm whipped out, finger outstretched, and he pointed across the room at Anthony Woodstock. John immediately recognised him as the officer with the jet-black hair who'd had the shifty bathroom rendezvous weeks earlier, and immediately decided he'd prefer not know any more about the guy.

Woodstock was in his late thirties. He was stocky and short in a way that implied great strength, and he had extremely full lips. But the thing that struck John was how he moved – slowly and deliberately, like a huge animal trying to conserve energy in the midday sun. He was mean-looking and had the walk of someone practised in cruelty, but in a bored, saturnine way. John looked at him, standing eerily still, staring up at the board on the wall.

Months later, John would sit down with Dunne over drinks, shaken by what had occurred during his second buddy period, and Dunne would tell him his theory: that Woodstock didn't even have a heartbeat. That his resting pulse was ten, and under extreme adversity, eleven. If he'd been with John when the van crashed and the occupants ran off, he wouldn't have run after the man in the park with his gun drawn.

He'd have walked.

Perhaps that was why Woodstock had qualified for police rescue. Back in those days, police rescue had a kind of stranglehold on the spectacular; there's a reason Gary Sweet managed to capture people's imaginations by rappelling down buildings. Clad in white and driving white trucks, they dealt with the most treacherous shit on show.

About twenty minutes after they started their first patrol John and Anthony Woodstock received a call on the radio. They had yet to have a proper conversation – they'd shaken hands, grabbed some coffees to go, jumped in the patrol car and headed out. John was having a private strop about again having missed out on a buddy of good pedigree, and was starting to wonder whether he'd ever have a partner who he'd click with, when the call came in summoning Woodstock to a police rescue job. VKG had his car number and reached out to him directly.

Someone had jumped off a cliff near the beach, and they were now wedged perilously on an outcrop halfway down. The VKG told Woodstock he was required urgently, and he confirmed this, signed off, and curtly told John to turn back around. John did so.

After a moment Woodstock piped up. 'Stop here. This is taking too long.' Once again, John did as he was told. Woodstock gestured to John's door, indicating John should hop out, and opened his. John climbed out, stood up, and watched his new partner head to the boot, pull out a canvas bag labelled 'Police Rescue', throw it on the passenger's seat he himself had occupied moments ago, sit down to drive and take the wheel. Woodstock turned the car over.

John was in shock.

'What . . . what do I do?' he stammered.

Woodstock looked up at him with blank eyes, his head turning a tad too slowly. 'What do you mean?'

'I mean, how do I get back to the station from here?'

Woodstock shrugged at this, and pulled away, leaving John in a side street. It began to rain.

He started to walk back to North Sydney, swearing to himself the entire way.

He'd left his coffee in the car.

12

FANCY A PINT?

The second day of their buddy period, with John still knowing little to nothing about him, the Ant Man (as Woodstock was called around the station) and he were on patrol in North Sydney. They'd met in the cafeteria before their shift, where John was now eating a questionable burger slathered in hamburger cream.

I stop short, and stare at Dad. 'Dad. What the fuck is "hamburger cream"?'

Dad looks at me as though I'm the dumbest guy on the planet. 'Paul. Hamburger cream. It goes on hamburgers.' Then, he rolls his eyes.

'. . . Dad. Do you mean MAYONNAISE?'

Dad sighs. 'Call it what you like —'

'NO! You can't just call mayonnaise fucking HAMBURGER CREAM. By that logic I could call peanut butter "creamy nutters"! Or salad dressing "vinegar wets"!'

Dad just shakes his head at me, and stretches out his arms condescendingly. 'Sounds like someone could use a double-armed man-squeeze.'

John was eating his burger when Christine sat down just across from him. He smiled at her, and after a moment, she registered him and smiled back. Problematically, however, John squeezed his burger, sending a plume of white hamburger cream onto his tie. Christine saw this and laughed, to which John responded, a tad too loudly: 'Shit! Got hamburger cream on me.' Christine, rightfully, looked baffled at the phrase 'hamburger cream'. John wiped it off himself, and finished his meal. Ant Man, who'd sat silent through the meal, gestured for the door. Within minutes, they were on the road.

John tried to start a conversation once in a while, but every time he piffed some small talk into the air, Woodstock would swat it away, turning his padlock-shaped head slowly to face John, staring through him for a brief spell, then turning away.

John was noticing a pattern: with the exception of Dunne older cops were, for the most part, weary and flawed. He had assumed he'd be awash in positive role models, father figures who could guide him over the sea of justice on some gorgeous metaphorical schooner. Instead, he found himself tethered to a desiccated barge with a slew of passed-out deckhands who knew where the boat was going, sure, but who seemed pretty determined to take their time getting there.

And as John was trying to think of more boating metaphors to succinctly sum up his state of crisis, the radio flared to life.

Pub brawl. North Sydney. Hundreds involved, urgent. Over.

'This is 6-2 responding. We're close by, send backup. Over.'

Woodstock had snatched the radio up with lightning speed, and for a glorious few seconds, life surged through him. He turned to John, and said something no cop would ever say to him again throughout his entire career:

'Hit it.'

John wasn't absolutely certain what 'it' was, but he assumed Woodstock meant 'the accelerator', so hit it he did.

A few short minutes later, their car approached the pub. They were heading along Alfred Street in Milsons Point, it was around 10.45 p.m., and the backup Woodstock had requested was already converging on the scene with vigour. Which was a good thing: for an officer, even one from Police Rescue, to be attending an epic pub brawl with no backup other than a buddy would be folly. The kind of folly that ended with two police officers being punched to custard.

Here's something John learned that night: police love brawls. They loved a bit of biffo. In time John would end up working with some of the more aggressive members of the New South Wales police, and they all enjoyed having an excuse to release some tension. John never really understood this: if he was tense he had *The Thorn Birds*.

But there were a whole lot of other very experienced police there, around fifteen of them by John's rough count, leaving their cars and surveying the crowd across the street. Woodstock made a point of telling John not to turn on the siren, and all the other cars had followed suit: they all emerged stealthily from various side streets like jungle cats, before depositing their cargo of officers. Coming in silent had twin benefits: nobody heard them coming, and nobody got riled up. Apparently the sound of sirens got people's blood up in a brawl, even more than it already was.

And on this particular night, there was a lot of blood. John and Woodstock joined up with the rest of the police on site at the Blues Point Hotel, and they watched from across the road. John had never seen this many people brawling at once, the sounds of yells and fists hitting faces popping and flittering in little bursts from within the swarming crowd. He watched the mass of people, half inside and half outside the bar, roiling angrily back and forth, surging and spilling over the outdoor furniture.

Few, if any, seemed to have noticed the police cars at this stage. John scanned the crowd, just as he'd been told to do back at the academy, in an attempt to find the ringleaders. The trick, he'd been taught, was to look for those who didn't give a shit that the cops had arrived. There was always a knot of people in the middle who, even with an obvious police presence nearby, continued to punch on.

And after a minute or so all the cops on site, having conferred and cast their informal vote on who the ringleader was, nodded at one another and moved through the crowd towards a tuft of ginger hair, from which a flurry of punches was issuing forth. The brawl was like a fire and this guy was its hottest point. Snuff him, and the heat would go right out of the place.

Many people simply fled, eyes bleary from booze, laughing or yelling into the night. A few got physical, which was a mistake. John saw one man, a hirsute bearded gent with black hair, shove an officer away. The officer in question deftly ducked aside, tossed the man to the ground and began to cuff him. And like the Red Sea parting, the sea of people parted and there he was, the man with red hair.

Problem was, Red knew exactly what was going to happen: he was going home in the back of a divvy van. His move was not to throw punches at the cops, or even to run. Instead, with surprising speed, he leapt a metre to his left and grabbed onto a tree on the nature strip. As both of his hands locked around the trunk he drew in a deep breath and started yelling: *'No! No! No!'*

'Yes,' replied Woodstock, who advanced, grabbed the man around the waist, and began to pull. John joined his buddy, the two of them wrenching ineffectually at the offending party. One by one, other officers wrapped up what they were doing with stragglers and joined in, until eventually, out the front of a now entirely vacated pub, seven police officers were engaged in a lopsided tug of war with a drunk and the tree he'd become attached to.

John, straining and heaving, looked across the street, and saw easily two hundred people, many of whom only minutes earlier had been running for their lives, watching the spectacle unfold in rapt silence. One woman, eyes half shut, swayed crazily during what appeared to be an internal battle with her desire to pass out. The unresolved cliffhanger before her, however, proved incentive enough to stay vertical. She forced herself upright and watched, spellbound.

Then, after several agonising minutes of fruitless pulling and prising, the man's hands sprang loose, and he collapsed into the arms of the police.

The assembled crowd burst into cheers and applause.

Woodstock, hands full of dissenting ginger, snapped his head towards them and glared.

And with that, their ramshackle audience scattered.

After bundling the man into the back of the wagon, locking it, and clearing the site of any remaining miscreants, Woodstock walked over to the now closed pub, opened the door, ignored the staff cleaning up inside and flipped the sign in the window to 'open'.

He turned to John with that creepy, deliberate way of moving that was his unnerving trademark, and with the slightest hint of warmth in his voice, simply said, 'Fancy a pint?'

13

OUT OF AREA

Once he arrived back at the station after half an hour of watching Woodstock knock back several schooners, John noticed that the assembled throng of officers who'd been so eager to get their hands on the brawler back at the pub became remarkably stand-offish. He was now familiar with this tendency and understood it well: the shift was about to clock over, and nobody wanted to be stuck processing a prisoner, filling out reams of paperwork when they could be heading home, or out. And Woodstock sure as hell wasn't going to do it. Not that he wasn't in a fit state to – the booze had no discernible effect on his sparkling demeanour – but he made it clear that, as the senior man, 'No fucking way am I processing him. Your job.'

So John, now clocking overtime, decelerated from surreal street brawl to office drudgery. He photographed, fingerprinted and detained the brawler, processing his paperwork and leading him to his cell. The drunk was cheerful now, thanking John and nodding genially to everyone he passed. 'Night, Red,' John said as he turned the key in the antique lock. 'Night, Blue,' the tree-clinger slurred back.

John watched as Red slumped down and promptly fell asleep, this formerly warrior-like man, in whom there was now no fight left. His job done, he walked away from the cellblock. Hell of a night.

But before clocking off, he checked his pigeonhole.

Everyone had their own pigeonhole, labelled with their name and rank, and twice a day, before clocking on and clocking off, John would check that of 'Probationary Constable: John Verhoeven'. The tiny copperplate letters winked at him as he fought back exhaustion. It was, as always, bursting with files.

But that's how it was for probationary constables: they got given a lot of extra grunt work. If you've ever seen a kid 'clean' their room by simply shoving the mess under the bed, that's what the lower-downs' pigeonholes were to the senior officers. The space underneath the bed. The cavernous grotto into which one crammed junk before boldly claiming yes, they'd cleaned their room.

If you were a constable in the country, and there was a hit-and-run in your area, but for some reason a witness lived in North Sydney, then you'd have to fill out a special form and send it on over, requesting that someone in North Sydney interview and process said witness. Coming down from, say, Albury to complete that one menial task wasn't a particularly good use of police time. And that's the kind of petty labour, the kind of asinine busy-work that found its way to these pigeonholes, and which was then filtered down to probationary constables. And as much as John might have *wanted* to ignore these kinds of requests, he couldn't. His sense of duty, as well as the rules, wouldn't allow it.

Another thing he couldn't do, that any officer wasn't allowed to do, was go *out of area*. Your precinct – also called a division – had very strict borders, delineations of jurisdiction that came down to postcodes. And if you look really closely at old street directories you'll notice that the dividing lines between suburbs are usually drawn down the middle of streets.

John learned this specific lesson not in the academy, but when he and Woodstock rocked up at an accident on the border of North Sydney and Crows Nest. They were greeted by a senior constable from Crows Nest station, who, nonchalantly drifting back to his car, told them he wasn't going to deal with it.

Why? Because it wasn't his problem. Because the car had technically come to rest on *their* side of the street. *Their* side of the map. John's first thought was that it wasn't a ball over someone's fucking fence, mate, it's a crashed car, but he kept this to himself.

And at Woodstock's shrugged behest, they left.

This impulse to look the other way on the grounds that technically 'it's not our job' was something that, throughout his career, John would see often, and with graver and graver implications. Certain officers were willing to go out of area, though, when it suited them. Woodstock was one of these officers. During one shift he decided he wanted a beer. From his fridge, in his apartment. Beer was everywhere, but Woodstock, John knew, wanted a beer at his place and his place specifically. The rub? He lived in Collaroy, a decent lick of distance outside their patrol area. And, becoming increasingly savvy as to Woodstock's character, and wary of what might happen if he didn't go with the flow, John quietly nodded and followed the directions he was given. Twenty minutes later, they pulled up at a nondescript block of flats and headed into a ground-level apartment.

Once inside Woodstock made straight for the fridge, where he pulled out three cans of Fosters, cracked them open, and slid John one across the counter. John held it, the cold burning his hand, and surveyed the space. It was alarmingly sparse, almost the complete opposite of the place he shared with his brother and Gaz. It wasn't clean, per se; clean would suggest there were things that had been deliberately arranged and put away. No, this place looked . . . empty.

There was a single couch, a two-seater, opposite a small TV. The sound of the ocean washed in through large open sliding doors, and a set of unbelievably large weights was propped against the far wall. And just as John was wondering who could even lift said weights, the answer to his question lumbered in.

'John. Dave,' Woodstock said.

Dave moved like a tank, seeming to roll his way across the room towards John, where he stood, looming, before nodding and taking the third beer that John now realised had been opened for him. Dave's huge pink hand engulfed the can, and he headed over to the couch, which upon meeting his backside swiftly went from double-seater to single-seater. Dave stared at the TV, which remained turned off, and sipped his beer with a disquieting slowness.

'Ant, mate. Another?' Dave turned his thick, taut head to eyeball his housemate.

Woodstock nodded and headed for the fridge. And as he was opening it, a woman bounded down the stairs, and ran straight for Dave, throwing herself in his lap, wasting no time in peppering him with kisses. John clocked her uniform and registered he was in a police sharehouse of sorts, all three of them in uniform, potentially all three of them still on duty, and two of them drinking. The woman kicked her legs out, giggling, planting one final kiss on Dave, before popping her head out from behind him and staring straight at John.

'Oh! Sorry! Didn't see you there. Janine. Dave's girlfriend. Housemate. Whatever. You right for a beer?'

John stared at the stunning young officer, a tousled Fay Wray clinging to her King Kong. He noticed her lips. And her striking maroon lipstick. And he remembered the cubicle door, and the impression left there.

Dave turned his head to stare at John, his face now flecked with maroon lip impressions, his eyes completely emotionless.

'Get me one while you're there, mate.'

John gulped.

Audibly.

14

THE PURSUIT

'So, Dad . . .'

Dad shifts in his chair as if he knows what's coming.

'Why didn't you ever say anything? About this kind of shit. The out of area stuff, the general – eccentricities. It seems abundantly clear you didn't like or particularly trust Woodstock – Ant Man – *or* Dave. Why not, you know . . . say something?'

'Something I picked up over time,' Dad replies, 'was to keep my head down in certain situations. You gradually learned that you didn't have to participate in this shit, but you didn't have to try and dob people in, either. Plus . . . they weren't bad people, for the most part. They just weren't my type of people.'

I eyeball him sternly.

'Right, so maybe they bent the rules. Well, not maybe, definitely, but when you're young and vulnerable and climbing into this world, you tend to go with the flow a little. Roll with the punches. Keep under the radar for your buddy period, until you're the observer, the senior man. Then, you make the decisions. Your moral compass comes into play.'

He pauses, deep in thought.

'Provided you have one.'

That very night, mere hours after saying awkward goodbyes in Collaroy and getting back to the station, after John sat there mulling over this potentially lethal love triangle he'd somehow stumbled into, Dave joined them on patrol. John suspected that Woodstock knew he'd figured something out, and as many guilty people do, had decided to hide in plain sight. After all, if he was worried and guilty about his indiscretions with the hulking Dave's girlfriend, why would he then request Dave's presence that very night on patrol? He wouldn't. That would be lunacy. It was kind of smart, John thought, as he started up car 6-3 and pulled out into the night, with Woodstock and Dave both making chipper small talk.

It was a hot night. All the windows in the patrol car had been rolled down for the better part of an hour, and whatever pretence of geniality that had existed between Woodstock and Dave when they all set out had been smothered by the humidity. John wiped his hands on his shirt before cracking his knuckles and tightening his grip on the wheel. The tension was palpable, and he prayed for something to break it. Late on a weeknight in North Sydney wasn't meant to be this dull.

At that exact moment, as if in answer to his prayers, a white Holden Commodore in front of them jerked suddenly, revved its engine and sprang ahead, as if making for a quick escape. In seconds, it was almost too far away for them to catch. John felt the car shift as Dave leaned forward, suddenly alert.

'Fang it! Get the fucker!'

John obliged and they began their pursuit. Flipping on the siren, he sped up and tried to gain on the vehicle which swerved wildly to one side then the other, before finally committing to the stupidest possible course of action: lurching right, ignoring the one-way sign and barrelling down an almost impossibly narrow alleyway.

Without considering whether he could successfully replicate such a tricky manoeuvre, John told everyone to hang on, clenched his teeth, and almost wrenched the handbrake up out of its housing.

Spinning the wheel like a man possessed, he began to yell '*fuck fuck fuck fuck fuck*' as the car swung hard to one side and drifted, tyres screaming angrily, until it was flush with the entrance to the alleyway. Taking a deep breath, he pushed down the handbrake, jammed on the accelerator, spun the wheel back the other way, and resumed his chant of '*fuck fuck fuck fuck fuck*'. And, much to his delight, like a snooker ball making an impossible shot, 6-3 righted itself and slid neatly into the alleyway.

Dave whooped and hollered demoniacally, thumping John on the back, knocking the wind out of him. John, for the second time in as many minutes, thanked his seatbelt for holding fast.

Woodstock was too focused on the escaping vehicle to issue any congratulatory bellows, instead staring dead ahead, pointing.

'He's close now.'

He then grabbed the radio, and called in the pursuit in a calm, clipped tone. John knew at this point that, as he'd learned in his short time as a cop, and particularly from the incident with Len Beater, his objective here was to push the driver of the white Commodore beyond his limits – in short, to make him crash before anyone not involved got hurt. The alleyway they were both hurtling down was in the middle of the city, but it was late and no one was around. Six-three clipped a bin with a metallic *pang*, sending detritus spewing back behind them.

'Dad! What if that was a person!'

'The bin? What if the bin was a person?'

I glare at Dad, as if this wasn't clear enough already. 'Yes! What if someone had stepped out into the alleyway and been hit? What if that bin was a person?'

Dad stares at me, blankly. 'But it wasn't a person. It was a bin.'

I suppress a laugh. 'Dad, you know what I'm saying. Driving like this has associated risks, yeah?'

'Paul, mate, he was getting away. I had to drive harder and faster, to push him, but I wasn't pushing myself beyond my limits. Except for the handbrake move, which I hadn't actually tried before. But in the eighties, the golden rule was make 'em crash. Didn't matter if they were killed, if they ran over people or, god forbid, bins. Whatever. You wanted your man, you got them. Police chases back then were, on every level, out of control. And they were awful . . . and exciting, too. And it's different now, thank Christ, but we had the run of the city, and this guy bolted, which you generally only do when you've done something wrong . . . So I hit a bin.'

He takes a sip of water.

'And I'd do it again.'

'So who taught you to act this way, as a cop?'

'It was a take no prisoners mentality, and I didn't learn it. By which I mean, I wasn't taught it. It wasn't taught at the academy, it was . . . osmosis. These guys you buddied up with, were at the station with, you absorbed this stuff. You absorbed the culture of the day. So nobody ever told me to drive like a psychopath until I got my man, but I was with a mass of cops who did, and who quietly rewarded that. Go hard, go fast, don't give a shit about anything else. We were always in the right, no matter what happened. Police were in the right.'

I might be mistaken, but for a moment, Dad looks a little disgusted with himself.

15

BUT WHY DO THEY CALL HIM ANT MAN?

So the cars zipped along, sending debris flying down the increasingly treacherous stretch of alleyway. And just as John worried they would lose the Commodore when they emerged into open traffic, he spotted it. The dumpster. A huge, rusted green dumpster, clearly from one of the restaurants that backed on to the alleyway, had somehow rolled away from the wall where it normally rested and drifted into the middle of the alley. Seeing it, the driver of the Commodore slammed on the brakes, narrowly avoiding a crash. John followed suit and 6-3 skidded to a halt.

Before John had a chance to appraise the situation, or ask what they planned to do next, both Woodstock and Dave leapt out of the patrol car and, as one, tore open the Commodore's driver's side door. John finally saw the driver: a scared young man, breathing very fast, hands still gripping the wheel, knuckles white. The next moment, Woodstock and Dave yanked him out of his seat and pinned him against his vehicle.

At this point, they began beating the shit out of him.

John's stomach dropped. All the blood drained from his face. This man hadn't technically done anything bad enough to warrant this; as far as they knew he hadn't committed any serious offences (apart from reckless driving, though they technically exacerbated that with theirs). And nothing, apart from an errant bin, had been hurt. John flinched as Dave sent his fist into the young man's stomach. He doubled over, crying, spittle running from his mouth. Six-three cast a spotlight on the gruesome tableau. John, nauseated, called out something along the lines of 'Come on, let's book him', trying to distract his fellow officers. Dave stopped beating the man and came back to the car, getting in, taking out his notepad and marking down the licence plate of the Commodore.

'Better let Ant Man finish up.'

Woodstock, whose knuckles were red by now, struck the sobbing man with a series of backhands, the final one sending the driver into the road with a horrible smacking sound. He didn't move. Woodstock sighed, and with almost no expression on his face, reached down and plucked up the unconscious victim of his savage beating as if he weighed nothing. Woodstock, a short, unremarkable physical specimen, then strolled back towards 6-3 with the much larger man, dead weight, tucked under his arm.

Dave leaned forward.

'That's why they call him Ant Man.'

'So . . . they just bashed him?'

'Yep.'

I glare at Dad. 'Dad, I knew this shit would come up, but I have to be honest . . . I wanted more levity from these stories. I know that might sound weird but I guess I hoped —'

'There's plenty of levity, mate, but I'm not going to leave this stuff out. It's important. But remember, there's nobody around when this is happening. It's a dark alley, and there's no mobile phones filming every moment from different angles, there's no cameras strapped to the cops filming everything going on. There's just us, and this guy, whose only real crime was pissing off these two cops by fanging it when we got close. But this . . . this doesn't even rate a mention. Not compared to some of the shit I've seen since.'

I sigh.

'But I knew great police who didn't need to lay a finger on anyone to get the job done. They'd have despised what Ant and Dave did. I despised it, too, but I was a junior, I was a fly buzzing around. I was a hassle, someone they had to tolerate for a while, someone they didn't trust.'

John spent most of the trip back to the station in shock, trying to ignore the crying of the man bundled in the back with him. And when they started to process the driver, who was visibly injured, John learned what a verbal was.

Dave and Woodstock had the man seated in the interrogation room, with John watching uncomfortably from the corner. He wanted to leave, to hide, but something told him being alone any longer with those two wouldn't do the kid any favours.

'So, mate,' Woodstock said, gently laying his bruised hand on the man's shoulder. 'Mate, why did you speed down that alleyway, if you knew we were after you?'

Dave sat across from them, transcribing the entire thing, barely looking up.

'I . . . I didn't see you! I didn't see you, I'm sorry, I had a bad day. A really bad day. I'm pissed, I was drunk, I didn't know . . .' the man stammered, shoulders hunched, looking like he was going to pass out from exhaustion, eye swollen, blood caked on one cheek.

Dave's huge fingers stamped away at the typewriter, with a sudden flurry of strokes so emphatic you'd think he was trying to kill an insect that wouldn't stay still. There was an aggressive *ding!* from the typewriter bell.

John wandered over to look at the transcript, and saw what Dave had recorded as the beaten man's response:

```
Go fuck yourselves. I fucked your wife, you fucking
cunt.
```

Dave looked up at John and placed a single thick finger over his lips, shushing and suppressing an impish smile all at once.

'Wait! What?' I sputter.

Dad looks just as mad as I am. 'Months later the man turned up at court, and the magistrate read his "statement" aloud. He was instantly convicted. Several months after that, I was driving beneath an extremely prominent, sketchy underpass and looked up to see, spray-painted in angry capitals: STOP POLICE VERBALS. You started to see it everywhere. Bridges, walls, gutters. Everywhere. And before you ask, no, I never verballed anyone.'

John finished his shift, shaken. As he left he saw Christine, that miraculous woman who kept popping up in his life, heading in through the double doors. She smiled at him. He smiled back. He wondered what she'd think if she knew he hadn't told them to stop.

He suddenly felt very guilty, and very homesick.

There is a lengthy pause. Dad reaches for the whiskey, and pours two glasses, sliding me one. He takes a sip, grimaces, then leans over and pulls a cord. The venetian blinds flip open, casting sharp strips of light and darkness across his face.

He squints at me. 'Does this look cool?'

And then it hits me: he's putting on a show for me, trying to ape Philip Marlowe. He's doing a shitty, adorable impression of a private dick. He's trying to impress me.

Which is exactly what I'd be doing in his position.

Maybe we aren't so different after all.

16

A MEET AND GREET

John was beginning to get restless. He was nearly done with his placement at North Sydney and he'd been buddied up with Woodstock for some time now, and as John had long since become acclimatised to, he was always the one doing the driving – perhaps the only thing he was still enjoying about being buddied up with the man. At least when driving John had some modicum of control over their actions.

On one particular shift, at around two in the morning, Woodstock picked up the radio with his callused hand and issued a very odd request. At the time John was driving car 6-1, a paddy wagon. The P-Wagon, as it was often called by those driving it, was the first response vehicle. If something went wrong, which it all too often did, it could hold any recently booked prisoners, be they drunk idiots or armed psychopaths. In either case, any corralled wrongdoers ended up sitting upsettingly close to you in what was essentially a large metal box. This is what John was driving that night.

And to adequately comprehend the gravity of what happens next, it might help to know the following.

Imagine there are five cars working a shift. Now, imagine if car A wants to have a social chat, off the record, with Car C. To do this, off air — and remember, this is long before mobile phones — they would hop on the radio and give a dodgy job. Which is to say, one that doesn't exist. This is what happened to John that night. Woodstock reached over, picked up the radio and said in a crisp, deadpan voice, 'This is car 6-1. Can you get car 6-3 to meet me at the south end of Balmoral Park? Over.'

John assumed this was a job of some sort, though he could tell *something* was amiss. He opened his mouth to ask a question, but the look on his minder's face was enough to quash any queries he might have.

'Quick. We need to get there quick,' Woodstock said in a curt tone, one which implied any questions would be met with stony silence. John checked his mirror, pulled a U-turn and went to flip on the siren. His hand was caught roughly by the wrist, and he was issued a shake of the head and an impatient sigh. John muffled the alarm bells going off, and began heading towards Balmoral Beach.

When they arrived, the park was completely black. The wagon peeled cautiously into the empty car park. John couldn't see much: a breeze kicked up, sending a Chiko Roll wrapper flitting across the windscreen. A dingy public toilet block sat nearby, the flickering halogen bulb mounted inside the only source of light other than their headlights. John made to park beneath an enormous Norfolk Island pine swaying in the breeze, but Woodstock pointed instead to a small clearing. There, in the middle of the inky expanse, was another police car: 6-3.

Six-three dipped its headlights on and off at them, then sat in the darkness, waiting. John knew something was powerfully askew.

Nothing good ever happens in a park at 2 a.m. This had the stink of something illicit about it.

John rattled hurriedly through his options.

Call someone? Impossible, the radio was being watched by Woodstock.

Refuse to pull up next to the other car? Impossible. He had no desire to disobey an order simply because it was both mysterious and creepy as hell – or rather, he did, but he found himself too frozen with indecision and fear after having seen what Ant Man was capable of to do anything just now. Piss himself? Possible. A novel approach, to be sure, but he had no idea how much paperwork would be involved, both in the explaining of and the mopping up of panic-induced bodily fluids. He resolved instead to just pull up next to the other car and see how everything shook out.

From the other car, two figures emerged. One hung back, leaning against the vehicle. Woodstock quietly got out, shut his door, and headed towards them. The larger of the two slowly approached Woodstock. John left the headlights on, illuminating car 6-3 and the other officers. Woodstock shook the hand of the senior officer, and the two of them headed to the boot of his car. John, concerned, quietly opened his door, got out, shut it and slowly approached.

The trunk popped open, and the two senior officers walked away, talking in hushed tones and . . .

'Drinking. They're drinking.'

John span around, already on edge. The driver of the other car was still leaning against it. He looked exhausted as he spoke, as if this was a common occurrence. He extended a hand. 'Julian.' They shook hands and began to talk. The real problem with all of this, as John would find out from Julian as their buddies drank beers in the dark? Not that the trunk of a patrol car was full to bursting with purloined booze. Not even that they were drinking on duty. The pith of this moral quandary, Julian explained under his breath to John, was that both cars were now well and truly out of area, which meant that *if* something really, really bad were to happen and these cars – one of which was the first response vehicle for North Sydney – were called up, all four of them would be fucked. Or would be were this not such a depressingly common practice.

John looked into the boot. There had to be at least two slabs of beer in there.

To John's mind, though, there was another pertinent question not being asked, so he asked it of Julian.

'How are you finding . . . you know.'

He gestured covertly towards the two senior officers.

Julian shook his head. 'Look . . . It's shit, mate. But . . .' He gave a shrug, a *what can you do?* look.

John sighed. 'I don't think I want to turn out like that.'

Julian looked up and smiled. He nodded, and found a more comfortable perch against the car. They stood there like that for a minute, sizing up each other. John wondered if perhaps Julian was a bit like him, a little more discerning. More questioning. And if that was the case, hell, maybe there were more like them, cops who raised an eyebrow at this kind of thing. He stood there, hoping that perhaps this cop thing *wasn't* going to be a descent into lawlessness after all. Then, to break the silence, he asked the one thing he'd been wondering since they'd shaken hands.

'How the hell did you get talked into cleaning classroom windows and wearing a wig?'

17

THE FLOATER

John's nocturnal meeting with Julian had cheered him up. It reminded him that he wasn't completely alone in noticing how busted some officers' moral compasses were. Rather than confronting Ant Man and Dave over their conduct, or pulling off his badge only to slam it on the desk of his superior before delivering some crisp riposte, John resolved to climb the ranks. To change the system from the inside.

Of course, one potential problem with this desire is that by the time you're at the top, you're so muddy from the climb you no longer remember what the bottom was even like. John didn't know any of this, though, and chose to throw himself into his work and pretend he wasn't now shit scared of Ant Man for their remaining weeks together. So when they were on patrol later that week and received a call from Luna Park, he saw it as a test of his fortitude.

John hated clowns. Which is passé nowadays, but before pop culture turned them into ghoulish van-demons who feed on children while quaffing helium and quaaludes, clowns were considered funny. As a child, though, John had been invited to Luna Park every year for a friend's birthday. Hancock was a rich kid and each of his birthday parties involved his parents renting out some of the park and inviting a select group of friends there for a spree of cake and free rides. One year, in the fifth grade, John had been on the Rotor, and while being flung around, looked over at the ghost train and could have sworn he saw a young boy inside, hammering away on the fence, screaming to be let out. On the next turn of the ride, John looked over, shell-shocked, but the boy was gone.

He went home sick to his stomach, and not just on account of the centrifuge and suspiciously wet hot dogs. And he forever associated that sensation with the time he saw something abhorrent inside the mouth of a giant, grinning clown.

So when the call came through at 1 a.m. that a body had been found at Luna Park, and he was told to drive to a place he considered mildly haunted, John thought . . . fine. This is fine.

Luna Park is nestled on the harbour in the shadow of the Harbour Bridge, and at night, all the shapes skirting the water look less like glittering buildings housing Sydney's richest curmudgeons, and more like broken, jagged teeth. The entrance to the park is a wide-eyed, looming clown head, mouth forced open in a permanent rictus to allow children to pass into what is presumably his digestive tract.

John walked slightly behind Woodstock, who was already making a beeline in the darkness for the security booth where a lone guard sat. John looked up at the colossal alabaster guardian of the park. The clown stared straight ahead. 'I'm watching you,' John muttered.

The clown didn't reply. John considered this a win.

The booth only had enough room for a single occupant, and

as John caught up with Woodstock, it became apparent that the curly-haired guard, whose name tag read 'Quentin', was, in fact, reading *The Thorn Birds.*

As if this night couldn't get any weirder.

The guard placed his book face down, left the booth, and began rifling through a key ring the size of his head. 'It's just through here. I haven't touched anything, don't worry.' Woodstock didn't look worried. John prayed this Quentin lad wouldn't give his partner any excuse for a beating.

The three of them, having cleared the gate, began walking through the empty park. John began to consider possible scenarios. Worst case: the place was haunted. He'd be found the next day, strung up and exsanguinated. Best case scenario: the park would leave them be, and they'd find a body. John knew from the academy that finding a body guaranteed one thing: paperwork. Lots of it. Odds were they'd be stuck there for an hour, canvassing and closing up the crime scene. Then they'd have to head over to the morgue. Then, back to the station for the forms signed in triplicate. At this rate John wouldn't be in bed until 9 a.m.

They reached the water, just near the entrance to Coney Island, the enormous old building that housed the hall of mirrors. An embankment of huge, sharp, ashen rocks veered down steeply for a metre or so before reaching the bay. Quentin pointed and mumbled, 'Body. Down there.' He covered his mouth so as not to be sick, tottered back in the direction of his little booth and left them to it.

Woodstock sighed, grunting as he stepped tentatively from one rock to another, then motioned for John to come and have a look. Stepping out onto a rock of his own, John peered into the darkness. He turned on his torch, and swung it downwards.

Wedged between two shards of stone and bobbing like a fat cork in the water was a body. It was taut, filled with gases, and face down.

'Dad, I . . . Why do bodies always float face down?'

He looks a little chuffed. 'Well, the body sinks once the places in it that on a good day are full of air, like the lungs, fill with water. That's a bad day, obviously. Then, all the stuff in your guts starts to bubble away and create gases, like methane, which inflate those areas and pull it up to the surface.'

'Oh, so the dead body is full of farts?'

'I'm going to ignore that, even though . . . yes, farts. So the farts haul the body upwards, but because there's nowhere for the . . . farts to go in the arms and legs, which are heavier now, the body will flip and pull the most buoyant part – the torso – towards the surface.'

'So what if your neck was broken and your face is facing the other way?'

'Then you had a *very* bad day. Now stop interrupting.'

John couldn't tell if the body was a man or a woman, but from the sheer size, he guessed it was probably a man. He just made out jeans and a mottled jacket stretched over the shiny, decaying mass, when Woodstock interrupted him with a whistle.

'Oi. Go find me a stick. Big one.'

John looked perplexed, hoping he'd manage to get back in time for a decent sleep before his next shift. Walking through the empty amusement park, he found his mind straying back to the corpse, its skin beginning to slip away from the muscles beneath. Beset by nausea, he quickly made himself think of something else, something pleasant. Casting about, he settled on the look he'd shared with Christine. He'd been thinking about her occasionally. He continued thinking about her as he cast about for a stick, before seeing a two-by-four leaning against a few crates. He grabbed it, sighed at their impending corpse-paperwork quagmire, and made his way back towards the crime scene.

The body had touched down in their zone, and was definitely now their problem. Bodies in the water were like balls that fell in people's yards: finders keepers.

John sighed again as he gave the beam to Woodstock. And then Woodstock, without batting an eye, stepped down, planted the other end of the beam into the back of the cadaver, and shoved. It came loose and slowly floated away. He threw the beam into the distance, wiped his hands, and turned back to John.

'Not our problem if it never landed in our area. Now let's get the fuck out of here.'

They made their way back to the car. As they passed Quentin in his little booth, Woodstock looked back, grunted, and gave a little shudder.

'Fuck me . . . Thought I saw a kid standing over there.'

18

SO SUE ME

John was about to finish his buddy period. It had been a long, gruelling twelve weeks, first with Len, then with Woodstock, neither of whom John would have chosen if given the choice. The energy around the station from the junior constables was palpable; everyone knew they were soon to be released from their designated babysitters and become actual officers. Once the buddy period ended, it basically became like a retail job: you'd come in, check the roster and see who you'd be working with that shift.

'Wait wait wait wait wait. Wait, Dad. Wait.'

Dad does as he was asked: he waits.

'See, I'd assumed this story was about you and your partner. And when I was growing up . . . wasn't it just you and Julian?'

'No, it's a story about me and my *partners*. Plural. We've been over this before, Paul, this isn't *Lethal Weapon*. This isn't a buddy-cop movie, it's shift work. You have hundreds of partners throughout your career. Take Woodstock, for example; he was a partner. And Woodstock was shit. Shit at his job, shitty attitude, dangerous. Shouldn't have been there. Dave was frightening, but was also a very efficient cop. Got results. The wrong way, but got them.'

I think on this. 'Right. So . . . when do we get to Julian?'

Dad mulls this over, as if trying to get timelines straight. Julian was, and presumably still is, my godfather. He and Dad were best friends on the force together. Julian was tall, handsome, aggressively confident, warm, witty, kind, and I worshipped the ground he stood on. I loved the guy. Dad was very emphatic that Julian took his duty as my godfather very seriously; he was always imparting words of wisdom whenever he was over at ours when I was a kid, which was a lot. He was an integral part of my life while growing up, and he and Dad were as thick as thieves, until I was in my teens at least.

'We'll get back to Julian later,' Dad says firmly.

As John was now entering the police force proper, his job was about to get harder. He'd be driving around a senior officer, but wouldn't get to make any calls yet. Answering a call? Not up to him. Hitting the siren? Not up to him. Burgers or pizza? Not up to him. Dealing with a body or shunting it out into Poseidon's inky embrace? Definitely not up to him.

They're the brain, he's the body. They're Kirk, and he's the nameless redshirt who dies when a vast and horny energy being tries to have sex with the ship.

John's first proper partner, the day after he'd broken free from the yoke of his buddy period, was Sue Daufin. Sue was waiting by the desk, and greeted John with a warm smile, a very firm handshake and a curt nod. She was John's height, broad-shouldered, and had her hair cut short. She had bright blue eyes, and John had a good feeling about her right away.

In fact, John was so enthusiastic he was literally bouncing on the spot.

'Shit, you're like a coiled spring. Come on, Verhoeven, let's go. Let's see what you've got.'

John instantly felt safer with her than he had with Woodstock or Len by a magnitude of ten. As they headed out towards the cars, Christine approached them, coming back from a freshly concluded shift. John smiled, went to wave, then thought better of it, faltering awkwardly. Christine headed towards them, grinning and waving. Fuck it, thought John. Take a swing.

He waved back.

So did Sue. She and Christine hugged. John lowered his hand and tried to dissolve into the floor.

After warmly greeting her friend, Sue remembered John was there. 'Chris. This is John, John Verhoeven, he's with me today. John, this is Christine, we were at the academy together.'

John smiled again, stammered something along the lines of 'I am John, that's me', and shook Christine's hand. She smiled and shook back.

'I've seen you around! Nice to meet you. You'll like Sue, she's very gentle with the new ones. I have to run, though, sorry... paperwork. Fucking domestic. See you for drinks tomorrow, Sue!' And with that, Christine jogged off into the bowels of the station. Sue turned and looked John square in the eye.

'She's on Romeo Squad, they deal with sexual assaults and juvenile crimes, the heavy shit. Hard woman. You'd like her.' A knowing glance, then Sue cuffed John on the arm. 'Car. Come on.'

Sue had a passion for the job that John hadn't seen in Len or Woodstock, and she reminded him of a stern but passionate school principal. By three in the afternoon, John was feeling far better about his career choice, and had all but forgotten the Luna Park incident. As they found themselves parked at a set of lights, John's mind was ablaze. He was scanning for clues that weren't there, desperate to impress his new mentor with his policing acumen.

Like manna from heaven, he spotted a young man sprinting away from the car on the opposite side of the lights. Here we go! he thought. Suspicious as hell, spooked by the cops . . . John's intuition was on fire. He had this one. He prepared to fang it.

'Look! Sue! Look! He's making a run for it!'

Sue turned her head, looked at the fleeing man, then at John.

'Sue! Do we pursue?'

A pause. John bounced in place.

'John, he's running for cover. It's raining.'

He checked. It was indeed raining.

John wasn't disheartened by his premature crime diagnosis, however. He was determined to do some real police work, and he was convinced he could still impress Sue in the process. Later that shift, he got his chance. They received a call about a tow-truck driver hassling a young woman who'd pranged her car. (John was sensing something of a pattern here.) He and Sue arrived to find that not one truck but three were parked by the side of the road, with the young woman arguing loudly with a gaggle of tow-truck drivers, inked to the necks they didn't have.

John and Sue got out and crossed the road. If John had intended to get first dibs on chewing out the assembled throng, he was too slow. Sue seemed to grow an extra foot, and strode angrily up to the largest of the men, putting herself between him and the woman, who looked relieved and shocked in equal measure. John watched as Sue swore blue murder for a full minute. The drivers were becoming louder and louder, and then the young woman joined in. Even if he'd wanted to say something, it would have been drowned out.

To that end, John drew his baton and walked over to the closest tow truck. He thought back to his previous tow-truck encounter and smiled grimly. This might be becoming a specialty of his.

The loud crunch that echoed through the street stopped the drivers, the young woman and Sue in an instant. Their heads whipped towards him, and towards the dent in the hood of one truck in particular. John's hand stung from the vibration that had run through him when he struck the hood, but he tried to act as cool as he could. He puffed himself up slightly, and glared at the men.

'Fellas, quiet the hell down and sort your shit out. She gets to decide who tows her car, all right?'

The lead brute whirled around to face John. 'My truck! You dinged my fucking truck!'

'Well maybe one of these lads can tow it for you.'

There was a long, tense pause. John looked at Sue. After a moment, she gave him the barest whisper of a nod. And then, after making sure nobody could see, a very subtle thumbs up.

'Dad, isn't this the same stuff that Dave and Woodstock were doing?'

Dad chortles to himself. 'No. No, mate, not at all. I never hurt anyone. If it'd been them, it wouldn't have been the car that got thumped.'

19

THE HOTLIST

Every shift, John got to the station an hour before he was due to hit the road. He headed up to the locker rooms, pried open his dinky little iron coffin, and got changed. He got his handcuffs and gun from the locker, too.

Later on, these precious and dangerous items would be held more securely in far more complex rooms with their own safeties in place, but for now, they resided in the locker rooms. This became a problem after there was a spate of break-ins wherein crims would bust into police stations, head to the locker rooms and nab guns, cuffs and, even worse, uniforms. But right now, John grabbed his and popped them on.

John would then head downstairs, check his pigeonhole, and find out whether he was rostered on as patrol, or stuck in the station photographing, fingerprinting, and doing the boring stuff. The roster was about 80 per cent on the road, though, so John didn't have to make a mad scramble for a free desk and get stuck into paperwork too often.

He'd also have to check his gun before going out on patrol. He'd been issued a Smith & Wesson .38 Special, a gun made for police at the time, with six bullets designed for the New South Wales Police Force. Later, police would be issued a speed-loader with another six bullets, but for now, John was stuck with a half-dozen. Six slugs per shift. John initially grumbled at the paucity of the ammunition being doled out, complaining that when he went shooting as a teenager he always had far more on hand. Later on, Sue would admonish him, saying, 'God help you if you need more than six bullets.'

After all of this preparation for the coming shift, John would next check the hotlist. He would sit down before an ancient, enormous computer which filled the back half of the room it lived in, type in 'HOT', then press enter. Central would wire all current crimes in from VKG in the city, meaning that this nightmarish, clacking series of computer banks would spray out hot, oily reams of telex paper peppered with tiny print. John would pore over these sheets, frantically trying to memorise names, locations and keywords, so that if a familiar face or licence plate cropped up on patrol, they'd be ready.

The hotlist didn't just get messages from Central, though. It was possible for messages from higher up to filter through. Much, much higher up, including the occasional dispatch from Interpol. Essentially, this computer would receive anything pertaining to the area that the station covered. Say, for example, an escapee from Norway has been spotted in Queensland and is seen heading down the Pacific Highway. It's likely then that he'll head through North Sydney. John might then see a message about this on the morning hotlist, significantly upping the stakes of his daily patrol. Now he had a Norwegian convict to roll into his day.

John would stand there in front of the clicking monolith, staring at the tiny cathode-ray screen, watching the machine vomit endless waves of paper, wondering how many terrible crimes were missed because of the sheer volume, the utter enormity of bad things happening every day. This notion struck him regularly, and he'd stand there awash in it. Then he'd inevitably remember that he *also* had to check the phone messages and the occurrence book, both of which detailed all the cases and calls that had flooded the station overnight.

Then he'd check the roster. John learned that checking the roster as an honest-to-god albeit unbelievably green police officer was like a lucky dip: you checked the board to see who you'd be tethered to for the rest of your shift. The day after his very pleasant shift with Sue – they'd bantered like old friends on the way back from the tow-truck incident – John arrived at the station with his fingers crossed.

He scanned down the board, and just as he saw who his buddy for the day was, a huge hand clapped down on his shoulder.

'John! Come on, you're driving.'

He turned and was greeted by his favourite mountainous Glaswegian, Dunne.

'I should point out, Paul, that Dunne had a troubled past. He was very senior to me, but there's a lot of baggage cops carry, and back in Scotland, he saw some shit. Saw a kid die horribly, shot while he was vaulting a fence during a chase. The guy he was running from fired blindly and took a chunk out of Dunne's leg, so sometimes on cold mornings he limped.'

'That's a great story, Dad, but what's your point here?'

'My point is this: having been through the shit doesn't give a cop, or anyone else, but *especially* not cops, an excuse to act like Ant Man did.'

John liked Dunne, and vice versa, although he did watch John like a hawk with the shift's first real task: getting the car ready. It was, John had discovered, taken as given that when a shift started the car would be prepared quickly and efficiently by the junior officer. John's job, before they even hit the road, was to check the car for faults and check the maintenance logs to make sure nothing had been done to the car during the previous shift. He'd kick the tyres – not too hard, mind. Then he'd check the fuel gauge. He ensured the batons were in place. And he had as much of the hotlist as he could carry jostling around in the back seat. In essence, John was mildly fried before he even began the patrol.

The senior officer would just get in the car and point. The junior officer had to scurry around making sure that when the pointing happened, everything was ready to go. This meant going on patrol, in-area of course, at an average and infuriating speed of thirty kilometres per hour. Essentially, you're fishing, trawling backstreets, sweeping for anything odd, with the hotlist, your torches, radios and all your other accoutrements in tow. It was like a road trip, with John having done all the packing.

One particularly balmy day, John was painstakingly sweeping and checking the wagon when Dunne loomed behind him, eyebrow raised. He watched John, muttering fastidiously to himself, and laughed.

'John, you look like you need to take a piss. Tell you what. Let's take the rest as a given, shall we? Hop in.'

John *did* need to piss. But he was so relieved and excited he didn't end up going for another six hours.

20

DUNNE FOR

John and Dunne were cruising around North Sydney, eyes sweeping about for any action. Occasionally, Dunne would spout a genial aphorism. John would mention that he wanted to be a better kind of cop than men like (here he would mumble), and Dunne would finish his sentence, saying 'men like Woodstock', and then sagely remark 'no man is an island' before apologising for deploying such a cliché in such impressionable company.

After about an hour of uneventful patrolling, they pulled down Berry Street and up onto the Bridge, when they saw a shitbox mustard Ford Cortina. John immediately perked up, seeing four young men inside who looked, from a distance, unsavoury. Dunne nodded, noticing John's instinctual reaction, and gestured for John to follow them.

'These guys,' remarked Dunne, 'are shitbags.'

'I know profiling is problematic,' Dad interjects, 'but as a cop you literally *have* to rely on it sometimes. Police work is mostly based on deduction and a feeling in your gut, and often it's in some way wrong, but you have to profile. And this was a car filled with roughneck crim garbage. These guys were up to no good. Body language, their look, everything.'

'So if you saw me driving in a mustard Cortina, Dad, what snap judgement would you make?'

Dad ponders *this*.

'I'd think, thank fuck, he finally got his licence.'

So they began to tail said shitbags, keeping their distance and observing their behaviour.

At this point, John and Dunne's car had pulled off a feed-road and come down a ramp onto the massive six-lane motorway leading away from the Harbour Bridge, and traffic was thick.

The difference between everyone else on the road and the people inside the Cortina was marked, and not just the colour of the car or the way it was being driven, but the behaviour of the men inside. The music, the erratic movements. They stood out. It was noticeable enough for Dunne, before John could react, to flip on the blue light.

The car, after a moment or two, saw the burst of light and awkwardly merged from lane to lane, until they could finally pull over on the side of the road. John followed suit, and with the peak hour traffic whizzing by, pulled the handbrake and turned off the car. He'd stopped just behind the Cortina and left an extra metre from the side of the road to provide them with a safe zone in which to stroll up and begin . . . whatever it was Dunne wanted to begin. Streetlights began to ping on as the sun gave up and sank over the skyline of Neutral Bay.

John quickly checked over the radio to see whether the car was stolen. It was not. (If it had been 'owned by Doris Smith, aged eighty-eight', for example, they would definitely have had something, but VKG reported it wasn't stolen.) At Dunne's gesture to the door, they both hopped out and made their way over to the driver's side of the Cortina, with John behind Dunne, making a show of eyeing the licence plate for any irregularities. Essentially, he was trying to look busy.

Dunne knocked on the window, and it jerked laboriously downwards. The driver, a young man with a shaved head and a handlebar moustache, laughed and rolled his eyes at Dunne.

'Hah! Right, then, here we go. What do you want?'

Instant alarm bells. In the eighties, as John was discovering, you didn't even attempt to *look* at a cop wrong without expecting some kind of unpleasant reaction, let alone a cop as imposing as Dunne, who often had to shimmy through doors sideways. Dunne calmly leaned in closer, and raised an eyebrow.

'Want to rephrase that?'

'Nope.'

The other occupants of the car winced, suddenly uncomfortable with their driver's bold stratagem of waving a red flag at this moustachioed bull. Dunne digested this. People who were this fearless towards cops, as John would learn in time, were proudly signalling that this wasn't their first encounter with the law. Swinging their dicks.

'Car's fine, we're fine, you can't stop us here. So jog on, copper.'

The driver had apparently chosen to double down. Dunne turned sardonically to John.

'He's right. Nothing wrong with the car. No grounds to keep them here.'

Then, Dunne pulled out his baton and strolled to the front of the car. All four occupants watched, transfixed. And as thousands of cars bearing commuters on their way home tore past him in a blur, he smiled creepily at the driver and brought his baton down on a headlight, smashing it to smithereens. Everybody recoiled. He put the baton away, looked down at the headlight, looked back up at the driver, then turned to John.

'Looks like a busted headlight, John. Which means this car isn't legally allowed on the roads. Which means, in short, these lads are fucked!'

He delivered that last line with the same kind of glee a footy coach would use to congratulate a team of eight-year-olds who'd just won a game by a single mark. And, just as cheerfully, with not a hint of nastiness in his voice or on his broad and frequently smiling face, he clapped his hands together and bellowed, 'Out of the car, cunts!'

John watched, curious as to how Dunne would handle this as all four occupants clambered out, all fight drained from them, and stood in a line. Dunne walked to the patrol car, reached into the glovebox and grabbed a large red sticker. He then sauntered back to the car, peeled the backing from the sticker and slapped it on the windscreen. 'UNFIT TO DRIVE' it read, along with some fine print courtesy of the New South Wales Police Department.

Dunne then leaned closer to the driver, a serene, diplomatic smile on his face. John craned in to listen.

'Right, boys, here's the deal. I don't ever want to see any of you in North Sydney again. Ever. So here's how this is going to play out. You delightful little gobshites are gonna start walking. You drive that car again, or remove that sticker, I'll have you all arrested. So consider yourselves lucky you got away with just a broken light. Do I make myself crystal clear?'

A silent chorus of vigorous nods.

Then he grinned, cheerfully clapped the man on the shoulder, motioned to John and they headed back to their car.

As John and Dunne got back in and peeled off once more into the furious traffic, John watched the four men tramp down the verge of the highway towards the nearest payphone, to call someone to tow their vehicle, which was now illegal to drive, or to call a taxi.

'What,' quizzed Dunne after they'd been driving for a few minutes, 'do you think I'd have done there had that young man from Blacktown, who was absolutely a burglar of some variety, been anything approaching civil?'

John shrugged at Dunne, and waited for a response.

'I'd have told them if they want to cause trouble they can do it in the next division, but not in my division and let them go on their merry way. Then I'd have called ahead and told the other lot to keep an eye out. But they'd essentially have got off scot-free, and I'd have been charming as fuck to measure.'

He gave John a wink. He was charming, John thought. Dunne lit a cigarette, and cracked a window. 'But if there's one thing I can't stand . . .' he took a long draw, and exhaled, leaning back happily, 'it's a smartarse.'

21

TRAINING

John digested all of this. Here was Dunne, a man whom John had an undeniably good feeling about, who had a fantastic reputation around the station, who had just done something a little dodgy in the line of duty. John decided that this was a line of policing he was more or less happy with: a wee bit iffy, but primarily good. Rough around the edges, yes, but with its heart in the right place. Two-thirds good, one-third bad. Not evil by any means, just a little dicey. Chaotic good. A little loose.

As John was mulling this over, cruising away from the car with the busted headlight, locking down in his head what kind of a cop he wanted to be, Dunne whistled. A single, shrill note. John, startled, looked over at Dunne, who nodded for him to pull over.

'Something wrong?' John asked.

Dunne shook his head. 'Just watch.'

John pulled the wagon to the side of the road once again, and they sat for two full minutes, Dunne perched there with an expectant look on his face as he watched the road. And then, as if by clockwork, the mustard Cortina with the busted headlight and the red sticker roared past them. Dunne smiled at John, shrugged, turned on the light and the siren and slapped the dashboard, snapped his enormous fingers and pointed dead ahead.

'We'll have that cunt.'

John hit the accelerator, the wheels skidding in the gravel verge, before pulling out into traffic in full pursuit mode, lights flashing, siren blaring. Completely intent on facilitating said having. Dunne did a little shuffle in his seat, keen eyes scanning for the Cortina. They spotted it and John zeroed in.

Only minutes later, John was once again getting out of the wagon, his vehicle parked behind theirs by the side of the highway. For the second time that evening he pretended to inspect their licence plate while Dunne waltzed up to the driver's side window, thousands of cars whizzing past them in a blur.

Dunne opened the driver's side door, the driver smirking idiotically at him the entire time. The smirking stopped short, however, when Dunne reached in, undid the seatbelt, and with both hands yanked the man from his seat like a tooth being pulled, swinging him outwards and slamming him against the side of the car. He held the man there with one hand, looked into the car at the frightened passengers and eyeballed them.

'Any of you lads down with this dickhead's behaviour this evening?'

They shook their heads, genuinely appalled.

'Any of you have the bright idea of getting back in this fecking car knowing it was now illegal to drive?'

They shook their heads again, with what John thought looked like genuine honesty, mingled with a desire to piss themselves the moment they got clear.

'Right. Then out of the car, and piss off home, the lot of you.'

Nobody needed a second warning. The car doors were hurled open, and the mustard sedan barfed its three occupants into the night. John watched as they hurried off down the road, fleeing as fast as their legs could carry them.

Dunne turned to the driver, who looked slightly pleased at the balls he'd displayed by hopping back into his newly condemned yellowy shitbox.

'Lad,' tutted Dunne, 'see what you've done is you've gone and ignored my helpful advice, haven't you? And look at that smile. Pretty pleased with yourself, are you? Right. Right. Well, you've driven a condemned vehicle, and been speeding, driving dangerously. You name it. So now you're going to come with me, and we're going to sort this out good and proper. Up you get.' And with that, he opened the door, plucked the driver out again and led him back to the wagon.

Once Dunne had opened the door to the back of the wagon's holding pen and unceremoniously punted his collar inside, he latched it shut and sat back next to John. He then directed John to their next destination.

John followed winding roads, up hills and down side streets, with Dunne guiding him. When John finally asked where they were going, Dunne smiled at him, and responded, 'the special way home.'

John prayed Dunne wasn't going to saw their man in custody's hands off and chuck him off a bridge. As if reading John's face, Dunne continued. 'We have a special way home, John. It's a place that we take people we don't like, and we take them back to the station via a . . . scenic route. Oh! And here we are. Turn down here, matey.'

They had arrived at Watt Park, shrouded by enormous Moreton Bay figs. By this point, night had completely fallen, and Dunne pointed to a small laneway. John pulled into it and drove slowly, the wagon shuddering up and down on the cobblestones. And then, as they cleared a corner so slight John almost missed it – he had to go back years later to make sure it actually existed, that he hadn't imagined the whole thing – an opening in the rock face loomed.

It was the entrance to a very old, very abandoned railway tunnel.

Or at least John *assumed* it was abandoned. Logic dictated that even Dunne, as loose as he clearly was, wouldn't put John, a junior officer, in front of such an opening and tell him to drive.

'Drive,' said Dunne.

So that's what John did. Their passenger was cuffed with his hands behind his back, sitting on a steel bench, balanced there by willpower alone. And the moment the wagon lumbered up onto the tracks and began driving along them, the metal box began bouncing about violently; faster and faster it bounced as the vehicle sped down, down, down into the darkness of the tunnel. John heard the passenger's body being thrown around behind him, and could hear increasingly frantic, panicked yells. 'Are we on train tracks? Are we on the fucking train tracks? Stop! Fucking stop! I'm sorry! Fuck! I'm fucking sorry! Oh shit, please!'

Dunne turned and yelled. 'Oh we'll stop, all right. We'll be seeing you.'

Dunne nodded for John to stop, which he did. Dunne then grabbed his flashlight, motioned for John to grab his, and yelled out again. 'See out your window? See the tunnel we're in?'

'Yes!' came the frantic, deflated reply.

'Good,' said Dunne, before reaching over and removing the keys, engulfing everything in darkness. He turned on his torch and began to walk away from the wagon. John followed. After about five metres, he indicated to John they should stop. They turned off their torches and waited.

They listened in the darkness to a string of frightened moans and pleas, and then several minutes later turned the torches back on. Dunne led John around to the back of the wagon and opened the door. If John had wondered whether the tracks were abandoned, that thought had clearly not even begun to occur to their prisoner, who'd decided, possibly while airborne, that Dunne intended to drive him into a train tunnel, park the wagon, turn off the lights and leave him there to be pulverised by the next city-bound service. This line of reasoning was underscored by the piss which drenched his legs and the floor of the wagon.

Dunne slammed the door shut. They reversed the wagon back out of the tunnel, drove back to the highway where they'd collared him and pulled the car over for the third time. Dunne hauled their foul-smelling payload out of the back, uncuffed him, and said simply, 'Fuck off.'

The man, less hurt than he was embarrassed, *ran* towards Neutral Bay.

In his report later that night, Dunne told John to refer to what he'd witnessed as 'some light track work'.

John felt as if he'd stepped into the Wild West with Dunne. As if he'd observed the grizzled sheriff with the heart of gold but a scary glint in his eye practise his own brand of frontier justice. The way Dunne saw it, he had sent a clear message without hurting anyone, or at least not badly. He regarded it as a slap on the wrist, proportional to what kind of a criminal the pisser in question was. 'Sometimes,' Dunne told John, 'you need to do things that aren't nice. Just don't go too far.' John thought on this. 'You don't agree?' quizzed Dunne.

'No . . . look. I struggle with this stuff. But I see your point. And I suppose anyone who voluntarily acknowledges there's a line to be crossed can't be that far off the mark.' Dunne smiled almost imperceptibly. 'Good answer,' he said. 'Good answer.'

After finishing up, and after he received a warm, friendly handshake from Dunne, John decided to check the roster before fronting up the next morning. Perhaps to be a little better prepared this time. Standing in front of the board he traced his finger down the grid to see whose name was placed next to his.

Christine.

22

MUM'S THE WORD

It would be an understatement to say that John made sure he looked good for work the next day. He was also early, even earlier than usual. He wanted to do everything he could to make a good impression with the woman he'd seen tease a shoe off months prior, an image he hadn't quite succeeded in scrubbing from his mind.

Hopefully, they'd catch something while out on the road together that was doable, but left enough room for banter. Something with intrigue, but without any tragedy involved. A dingle, perhaps.

'Dad, what the hell is a dingle?'

'You know,' he replies. 'A car crash, but a small one. A prang.'

'Dingle? Prang? Dad, please stop naming Muppets.'

At this point, Christine, my mum, saunters in. We catch her up, and she raises an eyebrow. 'Paul, I need to tell you about our uniforms. We had . . . well, we had no pants. We were forced to wear tiny skirts, and in early '81 myself and several other colleagues started an internal petition to get pants – chasing someone down wearing a skirt was idiotic, and dangerous. Their attitude was predictably backwards – as part of our uniform for patrols, we were provided with a tiny leather handbag, in which sat a snub-nose Smith and Wesson, .38 calibre. Same calibre as the men, got but fewer shots, and tiny. Needlessly tiny. We also got a small baton, between about eight and twelve inches in length. They said it was "ladylike". Every female officer I worked with shoved the damned thing into their locker and never took it on duty.'

'Why?' I ask. 'I mean, it's stupid, but it's better than nothing, I'd have thought.'

'Paul . . . if any criminal was near enough for us to actually be able to use such a small baton, it was probably too late for self-defence anyway. Anyway. The petition actually worked, which is why when I saw John that day, I was wearing pants.'

John had done his checks on the patrol car, and was waiting in reception when she arrived.

'Christine!' she said, smiling at John. He shook her hand, and replied (idiotically), 'I know!' Then he stammered, 'John, hi, I'm . . . hi! OK.' And they made their way to the patrol car.

Their patrol was dingle-free all morning, which left plenty of room for polite chatter between them. By lunchtime, the two were laughing at each other's jokes, an easy rapport now bubbling away as they swept up and down the patrol route.

Christine turned to him, smiling. She looked, John thought, as if she was going to say something important.

'Lunch, I think. There's a Maccas just up the road, in Cremorne. Drive-through?' I'm in, thought John. This is a date! Or at least, it could be. Now 'There's a Maccas just up the road' isn't a particularly romantic sentence, but as we all know, romance, when boiled down to its constituent parts, isn't actually romantic. It's clumsy, and functional, and it's all about timing. And it's a slow, strange process, made in fits and starts. So a nervous young man who'd joined the police force, a dangerous and bewildering profession, in part to meet a particular young woman, then finally heading out on patrol with her, *then* being asked if he felt like Maccas shouldn't have seemed full of romantic possibility. But it did to John.

Twenty minutes later, they found themselves parked down by the water, looking out at the ocean as waves lapped lazily at the sand. The windows were rolled down, and both John and Christine were eating their burgers – John a Quarter Pounder, Christine a Big Mac. John had decided, upon consideration, to avoid the strawberry shake. No more dairy-based explosions.

Christine tucked in to hers before turning to John and, in a deadpan voice, saying, 'I'm surprised you didn't ask for any extra hamburger cream.' She smiled, raised an eyebrow then threw him a sly wink.

> 'Dad, why are the burgers important?' I ask, genuinely curious how he could recall some details, like what burgers they ate, but be unable to remember others – such as key details of horrific crimes.
>
> 'Because it was a very good day, Paul. You always remember the very good days.'

A fine mist of salt drifted around the car, diffusing the light so that the whole thing looked like a scene from a soap opera. The car stank of fast food. The windscreen was glazed in droplets and there was a palpable tension in the air. And miraculously, as if some higher power had planned it, the radio stayed silent. They got to sit there together for a full hour without a single dingle cutting things short.

The conversation lulled, and John became very aware of how close he was to Christine. They made eye contact, and John briefly wondered what would happen if he leaned in for a kiss. He was, however, startled out of his reverie by a seagull, screeching so loudly he almost dropped his drink, and pinging off the windshield like a drunken helicopter.

And once again he became aware that there were people around, going about their lives, and a cop kissing another cop in plain view would be sublimely wonderful, but utterly unprofessional. What's more, there would be witnesses if he was rebuffed. Which, let's face it, was entirely possible given that John's breath reeked of burger, and he was a twenty-year-old man who hardly knew her. He reached for the Coke he'd brought with him from the station and threw it down hurriedly to mask his feelings, promptly swallowing the ring-pull that had come loose and was resting at the bottom of the can. John didn't want to throw off Christine, however, so he grimaced quietly as it slid painfully down his throat, then smiled at her. She smiled back.

They sat there for a time, just smiling at each other, before starting the car up and moving on. John and Christine had a moment.

And then, the moment passed.

So, eventually, did the ring-pull.

23

LIFE'S A BEACH

John and Christine got back to the station – which was always going to be the case, unless things went VERY well. Christine shook John's hand and went to fill out the standard paperwork. About a half-hour later though, she approached him again at his desk.

'So, listen . . . this is going to sound forward, but it's really not a big deal. I've been asking lots of friends around the station, just on the off chance they can come.'

John perked up. 'Come where?'

'Well,' she ventured, 'I'm headed to Fiji, on holiday. I have to go for family business, in about a month, and I'd love to get as many people here along as possible. Nothing worse than heading into, you know, family stuff unaccompanied. Basically I want a huge group of mates to turn it into a big party. So I thought, if you want to come along, apply for a little leave, I'll shoot you flight details and we can maybe get everyone together sometime next week to plan things out?'

It was hard for John not to read into the timing here. They share burgers, get along like a house on fire, possibly maybe almost potentially kiss (maybe), and then an hour later, he's being invited on an overseas trip. With Christine, of all people.

John tried to play it cool and mumbled something suave-adjacent (possibly the words 'Fiji, good, Fiji good' over and over).

'Also,' she said, 'some friends and I are headed to the beach this evening, over at Curl Curl if you're free.'

John was, it turned out, free.

After his shift, he raced home, grabbed a towel and some budgie smugglers, and shot over to the beach car park. The asphalt was practically molten at this point, and he'd somehow forgotten thongs. He hopped painfully onto the sand, made his way to the flags and saw several people lying about like catatonic lizards. John didn't recognise anyone other than Christine. Then he twigged: he was the only officer there. Had she even invited other people? Were they no-shows? He found a spot next to her, spread out his towel and lay down, skin so pale it was practically high-vis. She looked up from her book.

The Thorn Birds.

Needless to say, they had a fantastic few hours on the beach. John never asked her whether he was the sole person she'd invited —

'He was. Didn't ask anyone else.' Mum is in the room, a book in one hand and a glass of wine in the other. Dad chuckles, then she chuckles. And she throws him that sly wink. I mime a wave of nausea.

— but they had a terrific time. They lay there as the sun started to set, exchanging quips and quietly joking with each other, talking about whatever came into their heads. And before they parted John had mustered up enough courage to ask if she wanted to come to his place for a drink that weekend. And she did.

Saturday morning, John spent hours frantically cleaning the apartment. He'd also bribed his brother and Gaz to get them out of the house with a slab of beers. So that afternoon, Christine rocked up in a floral dress, with her hair up, clutching a very large, very expensive bottle of port. John had never before seen a beautiful woman holding a flagon before, and he expressed his surprise by attempting to refer to the port as 'starboard'. Christine was polite enough to ignore this, chatting with John about how she'd brought it from her collection, and this was one of her best. She then placed a massive bag of crabs on the table, and stated that she'd like it if they cooked them together. Perhaps, John thought, staring at the young woman and her offerings of an enormous bottle of fortified wine and five kilos of crabs, standing in his unusually clean apartment, I'm not the only one here who doesn't know how to flirt.

John did, however, learn that port and crab – if the crab was stripped, prepared for cooking, laid out and barbecued – paired better than they ought to, though he suspected the fact that he was falling hard for Christine might have been tinting the experience. Once again, they found themselves sitting very close to one another during a lull in conversation. This time he inched his hand towards hers, and moved in slowly for a kiss.

She lunged.

Which was when things escalated. John —

'STOP,' I bellow.

Dad looks affronted. 'Hang on,' he says. 'This is all part of the story, I can't leave out details.'

'Dad, details are good, yes! But details about crime stuff! Crime! Not about you and Mum, hopped up on crab and old person wine, going to town on each other!'

'Paul! It's part of the story!' Dad yells, now getting worked up. 'This is a story about Mum, too! And about how you were born, and what you meant to us! And I'm *sorry* (he delivers this 'sorry' like a sarcastic, surly teenager) if it makes you uncomfortable, but we had sex! There! Don't pull that face! So don't you *dare* leave this part out, you hear?'

Oh I hear you all right, Dad. I hear you.

24

I HOPE YOU'RE HAPPY NOW, DAD

And all of that on a full stomach.

25

DONE FOR SPEEDING

Things were moving very fast for John and Christine. As they lay about that afternoon, recovering from their . . . exertions . . . they both agreed they'd picked up on this, and after a brief chat, decided to cool their jets a little. Doing things slowly and being professional was the best course of action. Evening was coming, and they'd had a wonderful day but it was time for her to go.

John watched Christine leave, then after about twenty minutes was gripped by the urge to talk to her. He had no way to contact her outside of work but he knew where she lived, so without any hesitation he reneged on their accord and hopped in his car, started the engine, and made for her house, head still a little fuzzy from the port storm. He parked several blocks away and, his back sticking to the seat, began to write a love letter in the scorching heat.

He penned a series of ardent declarations, interspersed with apologies for so quickly abandoning their 'let's just keep things professional' agreement. Finally, worried he'd die if he spent any longer in the sweltering confines of his car, he wiped his forehead with the note without thinking, quickly patted it down before the sweat made the ink bleed, and began walking towards the house.

Well, not a house. It was a three-storey block of flats in Dee Why, where Christine was couch-surfing with her grandmother, who, Christine informed him, did not approve of her having much of a social life, especially not one involving gentlemen callers. This, thought John in his heat-addled state, would give Christine a balcony from which she could surreptitiously let down her hair for him.

It was as he approached the flats that he realised he had no idea which was hers. And then he remembered he wasn't even *supposed* to know where she lived; he only knew the approximate location because she'd made a passing reference to the name of the building while they were at the beach together and he couldn't tell her he'd cobbled together her address from piecemeal clues. That would be tantamount to stalking.

He could, however, slip the note under her windshield wiper. He could always argue that he'd put it there before she left at some point, and she'd simply not noticed it. He nodded to himself, went to put it under the wiper of her bright red sedan then hesitated. He walked back towards the flats, eyed the building number, then looked back at the car. He had to make sure he wasn't about to stick his innermost feelings on some random stranger's car. So he pinballed back and forth for a bit, before rereading the note, steeling himself, tucking it safely in place and running off. Not walking. *Running.* Like a sweaty lovestruck coward. She got the note, of course, but thank god she never saw his display that afternoon.

At this point, Dad excuses himself to go to the bathroom. He stands up slowly, cracks his back, puts down his glass and moves out of the room and up the stairs. I sit there for a moment before Mum wanders in again.

'Is it going well?' she asks, smiling at me.

I nod. She sits in Dad's chair.

'So was he talking about the love letter?'

I nod again. 'He just talked me through your first date.'

Mum sighs. 'I saw the whole thing. I was watching from behind a curtain on the balcony. He must have spent five minutes pacing between the building and the car like a dickhead.'

I almost gasp with delight and lean in to whisper conspiratorially. 'Does Dad know? That you saw him?'

'No! Apparently not! I just let him think he'd pulled off some kind of Thomas Crown-style love heist.' She looks giddy, sharing this decades-old secret with me. 'Paul, he looked like a drowned rat. It was forty degrees that day and his shirt was clinging to him. It took everything in me not to let him in and give him a glass of water.' Mum is laughing pretty hard at this point, then she pauses. 'Funny thing is, though . . . I meant it when I said we should slow things down. But watching him down there, it . . . It was very honest. I liked it. I think it sealed things for me. Shit! Here he comes.'

Dad comes back in with a glass of water, and Mum kisses him on the cheek and saunters out of the room. I wave at her, and Dad sits.

'So,' he continues. 'She got the note, and was none the wiser how it got there.'

Christine loved the note. There was, however, a cost to this caper – on returning to his car, John found it was smoking from beneath the hood. He eventually got it back to his place in Manly, though by that point, it was utterly shot. This meant that he'd have to rely on public transport to get to and from work until he could get it fixed the following week. And there's nothing quite as maddening as not being able to get to and from the one you're falling for with ease.

And he *was* falling for her. They talked every night that week, arranging times to huddle in phone booths, or spending as much time together as they possibly could without alerting anybody. Then the weekend approached, and John figured out that he was going to have to fly solo, as Christine was going to be up in the Blue Mountains working at a retreat for troubled teens. Because *of course* she was. She's perfect, John daydreamed to himself as he sat at his desk filling out forms in triplicate. She's doing volunteer work to straighten out the lives of young shitbags, he thought, and I'm stuck here. First weekend free in ages, and my fucking car is on the fritz.

Dunne clapped John on the back. 'Talking to yourself, boyo?'

John looked up, shrugged, then decided to hit up Dunne with a proposition. A favour.

That Friday evening, after clocking off, John was driving west in Dunne's yellow Sandman panel van, driving as fast as he could, convinced he could rescue Christine from her duties and whisk her off into the night.

And that's what happened. John drove up, snuck her away, boom, they were back in —

> '"Boom"? You can't tell me you borrowed Dunne's van and drove to a camp for troubled youths to steal this woman away in the dead of night without providing more details!'

'Paul, the details aren't what this is about, it's not important. What's important is that I went up there, thought of some excuse, I think maybe I threw rocks at her window. Something. Anyway, she checked with a volunteer friend who she'd helped out before and who agreed to cover her, no problems. We went back to Sydney and spent the weekend together! And she didn't need to explain anything to her grandmother, because she had the perfect alibi, she was away dealing with troubled kids! And . . . well. To say things escalated fast would be, ironically, a criminal understatement.'

26

THEY STOLE THE MONEY, YOU STOLE MY HEART

Even after their weekend tryst, John and Christine were still dipping their toes in. Not dating, to be sure; they'd talked multiple times about how they still felt they needed to keep things on the down low. It was hard enough for Christine already, what with being a police officer who had the audacity to possess a vagina, without the added pressure of people knowing she'd been shacking up with a junior officer. This was something else that John hadn't even really registered: Christine was senior to him. He was not only falling for someone out of his league, but a better cop, too.

So they agreed a second time to make a real effort not to rush things, and not to make things public. This was a pretty easy sell to John, in private, all loved-up with Christine staring into his eyes. But North Sydney police station only had a few women working in it. After arriving at work the following Monday, resolve well and truly steeled, John quickly became aware this wasn't going to be easy. He noticed that almost every single man working there was either making eyes at Christine or outright propositioning her. Once he even went to butt in, but she gave him a look that could puncture a tyre, so he stood back and let someone else chat her up.

They were, however, rostered on together the very next day. John figured he'd finally have a chance to show Christine how restrained and mature he could be about all of this. He wouldn't bring up the topic of them being an item, he wouldn't show any jealousy regarding the primates who fronted up to her every twenty minutes, and he wouldn't make any moves on her while in uniform.

To his credit, John succeeded at this for an entire ninety minutes. He and Christine coasted around North Sydney in their patrol car, making friendly small talk. And then, just as John was about to suggest an early lunch, they got a call.

A hold-up alarm was going off at a nearby bank.

In an instant, John's restraint evaporated. His alpha-male lizard brain got a stiffy and smacked him in the face, and without hesitation he hit the siren and pulled out into traffic. He couldn't help it – he was about to show off. Christine held on tight.

Problematically, however, it had been raining the previous night, which wasn't much of an issue when doing fifty down quiet streets. But as John pulled through a tunnel and rounded the corner in front of North Sydney train station, where several hundred commuters were heading to work at that exact moment, he turned far too hard. He pulled the car into a drift. As the car skidded he figured out that high-speed driving towards a bank robbery was a risky means of flirting, but one he thought he could perhaps pull off.

He could not.

As Christine gripped the dash white-kuckled, John spun the wheel in the opposite direction to correct the slide. But he hadn't accounted for a wet road, nor had he fully registered that he was going doing almost 100. With a terrifying screech, the car whipped around a full 360 degrees, hurtling down the road like an unhinged steel dervish. People scattered and screamed, dropping bags and leaping over bollards to find some cover. John yelled like a man possessed, instantly evaporating any patina of cool he'd worked so hard to accrue over the weekend, and pulled on the handbrake. They began to slow to a harrowing stop. The entire ordeal felt like it lasted a full minute, whereas in reality, it likely only lasted a few seconds.

Finally, the patrol car came to a shuddering halt centimetres from the side of a gorgeous Bentley. The driver glared, blind with adrenaline from the near-miss, and began to yell, then saw John's uniform and registered the car that had almost hit him. He still looked mad, and still looked like he wanted to clean John's clock, but the badge had the desired effect. He waved them past.

Christine fumed next to John, called him something to the effect of a 'fucking clown', and John meekly pulled away. If cars could slink, this car was slinking.

Distracted by his macho idiocy and ashamed of himself, he finally pulled up outside the bank. He turned to Christine.

'I'm sorry about that. Sorry. Let's just get inside.'

Christine stared at John and shook her head, more than a little pissed. She opened her door and stopped dead in her tracks.

John had been so distracted by their tailspin that he'd pulled up almost flush with the front steps of the bank.

The bank being robbed.

And Christine had stepped out of the car, in full view of the glass double doors of the bank.

That was being robbed.

John leapt from the car and crash-tackled her to the ground. As they landed, he wheezed 'robbery' and held her there for a second. 'Dickhead!' she barked. 'What was that for?'

This whole 'playing it cool' thing was going swimmingly.

They hadn't been noticed by anyone inside the bank, though. There were no gunshots, no yells, nothing. John helped Christine up, and they very carefully peered into the bank, to see . . . nothing at all. No robbery. Christine strode forward and began heading up the steps into the building.

'Wait!' John whispered hoarsely. 'Where are you going?'

Christine rolled her eyes and pointed straight at the bank, and at the teller behind the counter who was cheerfully waving, gesturing underneath her counter, making a 'whoops!' face. 'This isn't going very well for you, is it?' Christine said dryly. She continued her walk up to the bank. No, thought John. No it isn't.

Twenty minutes later, they were politely thanking the bank teller who'd accidentally whacked the emergency switch while reaching down to grab a pen she'd dropped. They waved goodbye to the staff, all of whom had been good sports as they watched John crash-tackle Christine in the street. They'd watched as Christine yelled back at John, then watched the two of them sneak into the quiet bank, then straighten up like nothing had happened once it became apparent there was no bank robbery. John had stood there awkwardly for a bit before making some perfunctory checks and, like their patrol car had done earlier, slinking away.

Later that evening, after they'd clocked off, they met at a hole in the wall down on the Corso in Manly. After a drink or two, Christine spoke up. 'I've decided to get a transfer.'

John was floored. 'When did this . . . When are you . . . I hope this isn't because of me.'

'Of course it's because of you. Today was . . . Look, I thought us working together *and* being together wouldn't mix. Shit, John.

Today they didn't mix and we almost hurt someone in the process. If that had been an actual bank job —'

'But it wasn't!' John said a little sullenly.

'It wasn't today, no. But this is getting serious, and it's just simpler if I go.'

They sat there for some time. John looked utterly crestfallen.

'So we're over, then.'

Christine rolled her eyes so hard John thought she might black out. 'No, you dill. I'm transferring so I can stay with you. We can't go steady and work together, so we just . . . won't work together. I filed for a transfer this afternoon. People will talk. People already talk. It's easier this way, and I wanted to try something new anyway. I swear, I did. And this was a good excuse to make the leap!'

John stared at Christine, a look of wonder on his face.

Now, utterly smitten and more than a little guilty, she lifted her glass and clinked his.

'You're welcome.'

27

DRINKING FRESH MANGO JUICE

John was still absorbing the fact that this incredible woman had plied him with fresh seafood and port – a losing combination, according to his digestive tract for the following three days – then, after a handful of other misadventures together, gone and got a transfer for him.

Christine kept reassuring John she was fine with the decision. John realised things were, once again, moving at the speed of light. He was twenty-one, and as green as the face of someone struggling to digest a slurry of crabs and old tawny, but somehow he'd fallen headfirst into an office romance. With guns.

The coming weekend, however, might provide a chance to exercise some restraint. Christine's trip to Fiji (the one she'd opened to the floor some weeks earlier) was only days away, and as no other officers had taken her up on her offer, it would just be the two of them heading off to an island paradise, after mere weeks of dating. John watched the days tick down and swore to himself he'd behave, and not be waiting at the gate when she arrived. He'd entered into this tryst trying to play it cool, and now, he was going to do so. Finally. In the face of all the romantic temptations a trip to Fiji would bring.

Three hours into the flight, Christine was reading Tolkien and sitting by the window. John cleared his throat, tapped her on the arm and she quietly put her book down.

'Christine,' he ventured.

'Mmm?' she replied, eyes still foggy from her ongoing airborne jaunt through Middle Earth. She took a sip of her water.

He slid the tiny box across her tray table and beamed nervously at her.

Of course she said yes.

'So then we were engaged. We got off the plane —'

I cut my dad off, baffled. 'Dad!'

'What?'

'Dad, this is such a big moment! You can't just skim over the details!'

He looks at me blankly. 'Well, she said yes. What else do you need to know?'

'Jesus Christ, Dad! I need to know everything! The airline! How she reacted! What you ate on the flight! Did she kiss you after she said yes? Did she hug you? What was the rest of the flight like? Did you discuss plans?'

'I don't know. Probably?'

I throw my hands up. Dad just shrugs. 'She said yes, I remember that much.'

'You said you always remember the good days. How does this day not fit the brief?'

'Maybe it's an altitude thing. Maybe it's the adrenaline. Or maybe it was so good it looped me back around to forgetful again, I don't know.'

I press Dad for more details on the rest of the trip. I want to know what Fiji was like; he gives me an evocative 'warm, it was very warm'. I want to know what they did for fun, whether they ended up catching up with Mum's family over there or not. I want details, because I am baffled he can catalogue stories about theft and murder, but for moments of emotional significance he has about as deft an understanding of the interplay between time and emotion as Woodstock did of compassion and personal hygiene.

I'm yearning to hear that they had a slow-burn thing going on, because it's a problem I've always had: rushing in relationships. Trying to cut to the good parts and shirk the little moments in between. I guess I want Dad to have more restraint than me. I want to hear about the two of them gradually ping-ponging their growing love back and forth. I want to follow John and Christine, and I want to punch the air triumphantly when one of them finally has the guts to lean over and kiss the other.

Honestly, though? It was always less 'will they, won't they' and more 'they will, obviously'. And then, before very long, they were on a plane. And it was 'I will', and then 'I do'.

This is when I finally get another thing Dad and I have in common: we're incredibly impatient, especially when it comes to telling people how we feel about them. It's a testament to Dad that while he got distracted from almost everything else in his life, he never had trouble focusing on Mum.

Sometimes, things really are simple. And that's kind of wonderful.

I still want to fling a glass of water in my dad's face, though.

Fiji was bliss, with far less family drama than John had anticipated; Christine's mother took the news of the engagement very well. And after they'd returned from their jaunt to paradise, John realised Christine would have to meet *his* mother.

Margaret, John's mother, was a character. Margaret was a public school teacher and a staunch Roman Catholic. She had unnaturally blue eyes, a voice that could cut glass and her bear hugs could pop the eyes out of any child ensnared in one. She was very loud, very generous, and very protective of her children.

Christine at the age of twenty-two already had a history of dealing with violent crimes, and had seen some of the worst humanity had to offer. She was also allowed to carry a gun around at work, and had once handcuffed a man three times her size.

Margaret was going to eat her alive.

Christine wore the engagement ring John had given her – a ruby surrounded by tiny, chipped diamonds, a ring bequeathed to him by Margaret and now worn by his nervous fiancée like a warding talisman. They parked outside John's family home, headed down into the courtyard, up some stairs to the front door and knocked. Christine gripped John by the hand, and he gave hers a reassuring squeeze in return. He felt like he was leading her up the steps towards a guillotine.

'It's open!' came a voice from deep inside the bowels of the house.

They opened the door and headed inside.

The central recurring motifs of the ancestral Verhoeven home were orange shag carpet and ostentatious crucifixes. A gaudy oil painting depicting a knight from the Crusades clutching a broadsword and weeping openly sat just above a sideboard, upon which an imposing flurry of family photos sat. Christine immediately saw a young, anxious-looking John staring up at her from various different eras of his life. It struck her that he looked just as young and scared now as he did back then. He squeezed her hand again and apologised for all the crosses.

'If I was a vampire, I'd be fucked,' she whispered.

He stifled a laugh and led her down the hallway.

'Back here!' came the voice once again. They rounded the corner.

At the end of the hallway was the bathroom. The door was open, and inside sat a huge woman with an explosion of frizzy blonde hair. She was sitting on the toilet, legs akimbo, pants around her ankles, and appeared to be taking a shit.

'Christine! Come, come over. Come here, dear!'

Christine's nails dug into John's hand. There was a terrifying pause. Then Christine released John's hand, took a deep breath, and made her way over to her defecating mother-in-law to be. She bent down. They hugged. Margaret welcomed her into the family. There was cooing, a shower of congratulations and much back-slapping.

'Welcome to the family!' she bellowed.

Then she flushed.

28

JULIAN (THE DICE WAS LOADED FROM THE START)

John was now engaged. He could hardly believe it. Christine had begun the process of her transfer, so John headed back to work. He was giddy. Over the moon. Exhausted. Frankly, he was ready to throw himself into his job.

So he bounded into the station, and ran his finger down the roster until it came to rest on a familiar name.

Julian.

'Fuck yes! Now we get to the good stuff. Why has it taken so long to get here?'

'Because, Paul, I'm telling you all of this in order. And good things take time. Come on, you're a writer, surely you understand that you've got to build these things up properly! Also, I know you always liked Julian. He was an honorary member of the family. But I don't think the Julian you grew up idolising is going to necessarily be *this* Julian.'

I make an 'eep' noise.

Julian was even waiting for him at the counter. 'John!' he greeted him, shaking his hand vigorously. 'We're on together. Fantastic. Looking forward to it.' John's immediate reactions were complicated. On the one hand, he remembered Julian from the academy, when he burst through a door to confound a room full of intellectually constipated recruits, a display of either commitment to the job and intense eccentricity. Or both. And he remembered their brief conversation about moral boundaries as their senior officers drank by the beach. He also sensed an odd energy radiating off Julian. Not like with Ant Man; this was different. Julian looked keen to get to work, an urge John shared and didn't see very often. He decided he probably liked this strange man, smiled and returned the handshake just as vigorously.

While John was tall and lanky, Julian was short and built like, if not a brick shithouse, something brick shithouse–ish. He was extremely fit if a little on the short side. He was handsome, with dark hair, dark eyes and blindingly white teeth. His uniform was always immaculate and he jiggled his left leg whenever he was standing still, which wasn't very often. He looked like he was born to be a police officer, and he warmed to John very quickly.

It's worth stressing this point: John and Julian clicked straight away. Perhaps John was still lovestruck and was seeing the best in people, still drifting around in the emotional foam of his engagement. What helped, and what this proved, was that when John found someone he clicked with, he fell for them very quickly. What also doubtlessly helped was that their first day on the job as partners was so eventful.

After some friendly small talk in the station, the two were on the road. It was around 11 a.m., and it was sunny. That morning there'd been a rash of break-and-enters happening all over

North Sydney. First at 7 a.m., then at 7.30, then 8 a.m . . . someone was flitting around the suburbs and removing people's valuables with remarkable proficiency. By lunchtime the two young officers had spent plenty of time lamenting the lack of 'real' police work thrown their way, and were getting wound up by this ongoing, real-time narrative of burglaries in their area.

And then the radio put out a call for assistance. The biggest break-and-enter yet had just taken place, and it was less than a minute from their current location. Julian and John reached for the radio at the same time. 'You take it,' John said, beaming. Julian snatched it up, answered the call, and they thundered into action. Moments later they'd arrived at the crime scene.

Along with everybody else. They cruised past the stately two-storey home, ringed by onlookers and hemmed in by police cars from surrounding areas. Evidently, VKG was so determined to stop this crime spree that they'd flooded the area with a web of patrol cars from surrounding stations – there were cars from Cremorne, Neutral Bay, even over the Bridge. Julian whacked the dash, frustrated. They slowed to a stop about twenty metres from the house and sat there surveying the crowd.

'How much do you reckon they took to get this kind of a turnout?' Julian remarked, eyeballing the people milling around the police cordon, as more cars came pulling up from arsehole to breakfast. From their vantage point they had a fantastic view of the action they were missing. John scanned the crowd, bored and annoyed. Which was when he saw the young man.

He was dressed quite well, in a cardigan and chinos, hair freshly cut, late twenties. He was walking down the hill towards the police cordon, and wasn't slowing down or acknowledging the crowd. But John immediately clocked a few things that were off, apart from him being the only person there who wasn't even looking towards the shitstorm outside the immaculately appointed California-style home. He was, first of all, younger than anyone else there by a good fifteen years. Secondly, he had slightly longer hair than anyone else there – this might seem like a small detail, but it was enough to raise the 'you're not from here' flag. John realised he'd just profiled someone based on appearance without realising he was even doing so.

'How clever's that?' Julian muttered.

'The cardigan?' John replied, leaning forward.

'Yeah. Rob a place then walk back and straight past the scene of the crime. Clever.'

John nodded. He and Julian peered at the young man.

There was a pause before John cleared his throat.

'I mean, it might not be clever. 'Cos it might not be the guy.'

Another lengthy pause. Then, at the exact same time, completely unprompted, they both spoke in unison.

'It's the guy.'

Julian laughed, and clapped John on the back.

'Fucken' oath.'

The cardigan briefly began to whistle to himself as he crossed in front of their car and made his way past two highway patrol bikes. Julian groaned.

'Cockroaches. Whenever you need them, they're nowhere to be seen. Put out a call for something exciting like this and they fucking congeal. You wait. Second this is over and we call for their help on a milk-run traffic case they'll magically be nowhere to be seen.' He strummed his fingers along the gearstick, restlessly eyeing the retreating cardigan.

'Come on,' said John.

The cardigan was walking down the street and had just nonchalantly turned the corner when John and Julian's patrol car came to a stop next to him. He came to a halt also, and looked up. 'Oh! Hi. Something wrong?' the man asked, in a very well-spoken voice.

John hopped out. Julian came around the side and pulled out his notepad. As they made polite small talk, they must have looked to any onlookers paying attention like two police officers chatting with a local about whether they'd seen anything suspicious. Yet John was fairly sure there was something wrong with this one.

Which was when John noticed the erection.

The young man's pants were standing to attention, the fabric of his beige chinos bulging out in John's direction. John felt momentarily bad for the guy then a little flattered. Then he decided to bite the bullet and follow his instincts.

'Sir, we'd like you to come to the station with us and answer some questions.' And bafflingly, in spite of them having no real grounds to question this man, especially not in an official capacity down at the station, the man in question politely, quietly complied. Moments later he was sitting in the back of the patrol car and they were heading towards North Sydney station. John could scarcely believe this.

Julian had elected to drive, and John made sure to sit in the back seat. His rationale for this was based on something Dunne had told him: never let a thief out of your sight. If the cardigan was carrying any purloined goods and John wasn't keeping an eye on him, he could shove them down the gap between the seats, making charging him nearly impossible. What they really should have done was call for the wagon from North Sydney – a vehicle which left nowhere to stow stolen goods – but John and Julian were on the same page here. After piling the man into the car but before pulling away, they'd agreed: they didn't want anyone else getting kudos for this.

That day, you see, they were working out of Mosman, which was a small sub-station, a low-rent offshoot of the North Sydney station. Every couple of weeks you'd have to hop over to the adjacent suburb and operate out of a sister station that was smaller and looked down upon. Mosman tended to get the shittier jobs, and the glory boys working over at North Sydney tended to yank the big collars away from Mosman for themselves. Calling for a wagon would have meant tacitly putting this potential suspect in the hands of someone else. So when John and Julian walked their cardigan through the doors at Mosman and explained to their station officer for the shift – a man named Ted – what they were doing, his perpetual simmering resentment at having credit taken away and his read of John and Julian as enterprising young blokes with good heads on their shoulders overrode his desire to follow protocol. 'All right, fuck it,' he said. 'Back room, quickly.' He gestured down the hallway. And so they went.

The room was just like those you've seen in the movies. A small, plain white table, soundproof walls, a typewriter, several chairs. They all sat down, and after a few minutes of polite chat with the cardigan, John and Julian learned a great deal more than they'd anticipated.

First off, he was nice. Very nice. Which might seem extraneous, but character goes a long way when you're assessing someone's guilt. He was from the eastern suburbs, near Rose Bay, and his father owned a very well-known jewellery store in the Strand Arcade. High-end stuff. Eventually, John cut to the chase, and, not unkindly, ventured, 'Is there anything you'd like to tell us?'

When he said no, Julian informed the young man that they'd now have to search him. They then had him stand with his hands against the wall and his back to them and began to pat him down. After searching him up and down, and finding nothing, John once again eyed the still buoyant erection. He cleared his throat, looked at Julian, looked back at the erection, and decided to roll the dice.

He stepped forward and closed his hands around . . . a jangling mass of metal.

'Sir . . . please remove your pants,' John said, now practically humming with adrenaline at his detective-grade intuition, and his relief at not having just closed his hands around a suspect's dick.

Within moments the interview table was covered in an array of immaculate jewellery. The young man was so relieved to no longer have the stolen rings, necklaces and gems jostling his balls, and to no longer have to hide what he'd done, that he was decidedly lighter in his demeanour. And much in the way that a long-practised menial task can distract someone from trauma, so too was the man lost in the task of arranging each stolen piece into piles based on where he stole them. There on the table, a glittering map of each burglary was laid out – a diamond ring and three necklaces from here, a pendant from there, and finally a mass of assorted jewellery from the place they'd spotted him, as well as a roll of bills. The young man seemed happy enough talking them through what made certain pieces more valuable than others, manipulating them lovingly with a practised hand under the lights, sharing with them titbits on how they were crafted. He seemed happy getting lost in the finer points of how the stones were cut, and in his mind's eye, John could imagine him working in his dad's shop down at the Strand Arcade. He thought about his own dad, Henk, and wondered if they could have ever ended up working together. He suddenly felt very sad, and very young.

All in all, there were easily sixty pieces of jewellery there. He'd had close to a quarter of a million dollars' worth of jewels next to his jewels.

> Dad lights up here. I've not mentioned this yet, but I should point out that for the past twenty years, he's been an antique dealer and valuer of fine arts, and a damned good one. Every year he pores over catalogues from auction houses the world over, memorising prices and valuations. He applied his eye for detail – honed while in the police force – to his new profession. So he leans forward and says 'one of these pieces . . . knowing what I know now . . . had a six carat emerald beset by diamonds. Today's money? Three or four hundred thousand dollars. Minimum.'
>
> I am reeling. This was a staggering series of robberies carried out by someone who knew what the most valuable pieces were, because they'd been raised by an expert jeweller.
>
> I wonder whether this heister ever thought about how different he'd turned out from his dad, too.

At no point did it occur to John or Julian to head out and tell anyone to call off the massive grid of officers from (as we've established, but it bears repeating) arsehole to breakfast because they'd caught the guy. These two were ambitious. John wanted to make big collars with someone who felt the same way as him, and, as the two of them had worked seamlessly in easing information from their suspect, their eyes gleaming, it became apparent that Julian was the partner he'd been looking for since he joined the force. They could do great things together. And what a score! What a stunning haul to kick off what he knew, deep down, would be an amazing career. And they'd done it without an ounce of cruelty towards the young man who sat before them. They'd talked it out of him.

And he'd volunteered more than they'd bargained for, too. He explained that he was struggling with an ongoing drug problem, and that he figured taking stuff from a well-off suburb would hurt people less. He explained that he didn't want to steal from his dad's stock. He owned up to everything, and he did so clearly, politely, and regularly asked if they needed him to repeat anything. He apologised, but he didn't feel sorry for himself. In the end, John and Julian found themselves feeling bad for the guy. They excused themselves, locked the door and headed back out to ask Ted for advice.

Ted was impressed. Beyond impressed. There was a rub, though. 'Guys, this is . . . It's great. But this is a detective's brief. He's gonna be charged with an indictable offence. Wouldn't be if it was just a few pieces, but the value of the goods pushes this way, way out of your league and right upstairs. Glory boys get this.' He looked sorry, too, and could see how utterly gutted John and Julian both were. He spoke up again, and gestured back towards the interview room. 'I'll call them, but I'll give you another hour. So you can get what you can. If you can crack it by then, great. You'll get *some* credit, at least . . . getting an itemised list from the perp with which jewels came from where would be quite the achievement. You could impress some big names that way. Otherwise, the detectives have it.' John, without meaning to, rubbed his hands together.

John and Julian had a hushed pow-wow before their next move. In order to try to weave themselves, and their accomplishments, into the narrative of this case, they resolved to take the now totally compliant suspect on a tour. They bundled him back into the car, and he then took them from burgled house to burgled house, itemising every single thing he stole from each one. He even took them past places where nobody had been home, meaning robberies in his spree that nobody, not even the cops, knew about yet.

John was frantically trying to take notes for later on, so they could line up each list with what they had back in evidence. The information flowed from him freely, and once they'd returned to the station he looked as if he'd taken a very long piss he'd been holding on to for days on end. Here he was, with two nice young officers, and he finally had all his cards on the table. No more secrets.

They sat back down, and John said those nerve-racking words: 'We'd like to get a statement from you. On the record.' Up until this point, it had felt friendly, confessional. But now they were about to officially stamp the case as theirs, still with some time to spare before their hour was up. The cardigan, sensing this was a big moment, and perhaps sensing that his future was on the line, asked for a phone call.

Julian, politely and without missing a beat, said, 'No, no phone call, mate.' He knew that if this guy got his phone call, he'd get onto a lawyer, and once that happened, game over. It was illegal, but Julian figured it was best to gently shunt him away from that option. The cardigan looked at Julian, then at John, then thought a moment. And finally, he smiled. 'Fine. What's the harm, I've come this far. Yeah, I'll give you a statement.'

John couldn't believe it. A suspect in a massive jewellery heist was somehow willing to forgo legal entanglements, and was going to officially throw this entire collar in the hands of himself and Julian, two rookie cops, on their first time out together. This was fate. This was incredible. Cardigan cleared his throat, and Julian, eyes on fire with anticipation, readied his hands on the typewriter.

And that's the exact moment the glory boys burst into the room.

29

THE BOYS ARE BACK IN TOWN

'All right, cockheads, let him have his phone call.'

The lead detective, a man with a ponytail and a film of sweat on his face, erupted into the room chest-first. His cohort, who had dead eyes and the loping gait of a gorilla with ideas above its station, trailed in behind him. Both wore ill-fitting suits. Both looked like they were a whisper away from punching John and Julian through the adjoining wall.

John ventured a 'But he was about to —' before the gorilla cut him off. John wondered if this gorilla was related to the one he saw across from him in the study room at the academy. For a brief moment, he could have sworn the man actually *was* a gorilla, his suit suddenly snug, his knuckles dragging on the lino floor.

'We were watching just now, we don't give a shit. Not your case any more. He gets his phone call, and you can get the fuck out.'

John looked over at Julian, his heart racing. For the briefest of moments, he could have sworn Julian was going to deck the ponytail. Thankfully, Julian stood up and grabbed the notepad with the details from their tour of the robbery sites. Ponytail yanked it from his hand and brandished a finger towards the door. John and

Julian filed out. The door slammed behind them, and feeling more than a little hard done by, they rushed over to Ted.

'Sorry, lads. They got here early, no idea how they found out.' John smiled weakly. He and Julian decided to stick around for a bit, out of sight if possible, to see how things washed out.

Here, then, is how things washed out.

First, the primates who'd burst in had ensured that Cardigan was allowed his phone call. He made this call to his father, who naturally insisted he lawyer up, and also that he refuse to give a statement, meaning the litany of kudos John and Julian were due for was about to get burned to a crisp.

Secondly, the glory boys justified their nickname by taking credit for the collar. As everything John and Julian had done so far was off the record, this was easy; John would later go through the paperwork and see no sign of himself or his new partner.

The final insult, however, was the worst. Eventually, the two of them left and resumed their shift back out on patrol. Several days after that they were tasked with taking Cardigan over to the District Court where he was being tried for robbery (a significantly trickier process, now that his confession was off the table). They decided not to poke the bear and avoided grilling him on the way over, but by the end of the drive, all three of them were laughing and joking and telling stories. Yet again, they were reminded of how much they liked this guy.

And after checking Cardigan in to the courthouse, Julian had the bright idea of calmly asking if he could see the charge book, an enormous tome which detailed, in tiny precise handwriting, exactly what each person present was being charged with. Julian scanned down the page and suddenly stopped. All the blood drained from his face. He gulped, his mouth hung open, and pointed to the open page before walking off like a man suffering a recent loss. John, puzzled, headed over to the book and began to read.

There, next to 'on such-and-such a day, in the year of our Lord, under 14-7 of the Crimes Act, pursuant to' et cetera, et cetera, was the section detailing the total value of what had been stolen.

That figure was $3000.

It was John's turn to go pale. 'Oh, shit.'

They headed back to the station in grim silence. After a spell, during which they fumed between themselves, Julian suggested they go over the heads of the two detectives who'd pinched their collar to speak with someone senior over at the detectives' office. After all, he reasoned, they'd effectively done detective work, and that would be a hell of a thing to work towards. Wasn't that the dream? General duties were fine, Julian reasoned, but they both clearly got a rush from solving crimes. Isn't that what they wanted? To end up as detectives?

'Well . . . yes. I guess so, yeah,' John admitted. And surely, replied Julian, they can't *all* be that bad, right?

So they drove up to the bleak grey cement titan that housed the detective division and strode inside. They asked to see the senior detective, making their way up to his office via the stairs. The looks thrown at them by various other detectives as they passed were downright predatory. Then before they knew it, the two bright-eyed fledgling police officers in crisp blue uniforms were led into a waiting area, then finally ushered into an office. The found themselves standing before a grizzled, craggy nightmare of a senior detective.

'What do you want?' he drawled.

John spoke up. He explained that they'd arrested the cardigan the other day, and then he described how close they'd got to a collar, and he described the two detectives who'd spoiled it, snatched it away from them. He admitted it wasn't theirs, but he went on to detail how they'd lined up the suspect for a full confession. It was Julian's turn to look mildly awestruck as John stood there, spilling his guts in front of a man for whom spilling guts could have been a hobby, if not a calling. Finally, John reached the charge book part of the story, and began. 'So we looked at the charge book this morning, and . . . there's a bit of a problem.'

This caught the man's attention. He stood up and leaned over his desk.

'Problem.'

'Yeah. This guy had close to a quarter of a million dollars' worth of jewellery. He also had a roll of hundreds which totalled five thousand at least, which he kept right up near his . . .'

'Near his what?'

'Jewels. So there's . . . a bit of a discrepancy.'

The three of them stood there. Cigarette smoke filled the office. A cheap clock picked and pocked away to itself on the wall, next to a photo of the detective shaking hands with someone who appeared to be an ex-prime minister. Finally, the detective spoke.

'There's no discrepancy. Now get the fuck out of my office.'

Julian stepped forward to speak and was immediately silenced.

'Don't, cunts. Out.'

And that was it. They headed back out, sneered at by several detectives they passed. By the time they got back to their car, they felt as if the entire grubby encounter had left some kind of oily film on them. They got in and put their belts on, neither of them quite ready to drive. They continued to sit in stunned silence.

'Fuck that noise,' said Julian, piping up. 'I am never going to go there.'

John nodded. 'Well hopefully we won't have to go back in there anytime soon —'

'No,' corrected Julian, 'I mean I'm never going to *go* there. To end up like that. If that's being a detective, fuck it. I'm not *ever* gonna be like that.'

He sat there fuming, then glared at John.

John smiled.

'Right, well, me neither.'

Julian smiled back.

Then they shook hands on it.

They were a unit now.

30

UNDER A FULL MOON

If there was a better way for two people who just started working together to become fast friends and unite against a common foe in a single day than *The Case of the Cardigan and the Jewellery Penis* (Julian's choice of words), John couldn't think of it. That same week, he and Julian had a fortuitous three shifts together. Between these shifts, he was helping Christine with her transfer paperwork. Not that she needed it; he seemed to have just proposed to the single most capable officer in the entire station. Being able to then team up with a new partner with whom he felt a deep, sincere simpatico made the process of losing Christine to another station far easier.

Julian continued to fume about their treatment at the hands of the detectives. On the clock, off the clock; Julian kept reiterating that he and John needed to go in the opposite direction of those 'platinum arseholes', to be the kinds of cops that took tiny shortcuts if they had to, but that paid attention, didn't trample all over cases, and who were, above all, kind whenever possible. During one shift, he pulled John aside and introduced him to Richie O'Neill, a friend of his who'd just been moved to North Sydney. John recalled seeing him around at the academy. Richie was a guy who Julian stressed was 'one of the good ones'. He had a broad, kind face, brown hair, brown eyes, and was extremely well spoken. Julian and he convinced John to grab a drink with them after work, and before long, the three of them were as thick as thieves.

One Friday night, after a quick dinner with Christine, John headed out to drinks at a club in Manly with Julian and Richie, with Christine's blessing. She had some reading she wanted to get done and told John to have fun. By 9 p.m., he and his two new friends were blitzed.

Manly was an intense place to get drunk. Many of the good bars were right up against the ocean – none of them was particularly good, but there were big ones, and sometimes a mass of people yelling can baffle a drunk person into assuming the joint is jumping. So if it was cold outside and, say, John and his friends were utterly wrecked from a night partying, they could stagger across the road and be on the sand with the black waves and the blacker horizon flinging blankets of salt water into their faces. It's an incredible way to sober up, as John already knew.

But when they got to the disco, near one side of Manly Corso and throbbing with drunks, John suspected it would take a lot more than salt water to sober him up. The three of them headed inside and made for a corner booth, where they began necking tinnies at a rate of knots. Music blared and people necked on in the flashing, pulsing room. The trio had set out with the intention of dancing, but before long they got onto the subject of the detectives, and policing, and their shared vision for what good policing should look like. As the drinks stacked up around them, their opinions became louder and more declarative, until before long, the three of them looked like three maggoted musketeers, arms flung around each other, *cheers*-ing aggressively and assuring each other that they would be better.

Finally, at 2 a.m. they staggered into the ocean spray. It woke them up, but they were, not to put too fine a point on it, absolutely pissed. Pissed as newts. Richie shook himself out of his daze, and gestured for them to follow him to a payphone. Julian stood there swaying while Richie fumbled in some coins and slurred into the receiver. 'You know,' said Julian, 'I think things are gonna be fine. This is gonna be great, this.'

John looked at him quizzically.

'This,' Julian repeated, pointing first at himself, then John, then Richie. 'This is going to be good police.'

Richie put the phone down, gave a thumbs up, and with great effort stammered, 'I got us a ride.'

Less than ten minutes later, Iver – a friend of Richie's, and a fellow cop – rocked up in his car. Iver was a cheerful teetotaller who had offered Richie his car and his driving services from time to time, something he informed John and Julian he was exceptionally deft at as he used to drive the police commissioner around. He was, as he made a point of saying several times on the way out of Manly, a 'precision driver'. He was also generous; he volunteered his services because, to be honest, it made him happy to do so, especially since he had trouble sleeping anyway and was pleased for the distraction. Julian then began to sing 'when I'm fucked I call Iver the Driver' to the tune of 'I Got You' by Split Enz. Iver seemed to like this a great deal, and joined in.

At this point, Julian drew a large, odd-looking key from the pocket of his puffer jacket and dangled it at John.

'What's that?' John slurred.

'Oh! Oh, you are going to love this, John. Shh, shh, everyone. Iver. Iver? Iver pull up at these lights.'

Julian patted the back of Iver's seat gleefully, giddily trying to rob the adult in front of him of anything resembling sleep. Iver pulled up at the lights, and Julian leapt from the car. They were at a quiet intersection up the top of Sydney Road, and John watched as Julian scampered like a child on a sugar high to the large silver box at the base of the traffic lights. He popped it open, inserted the key, and turned it. And sure enough . . .

The lights, previously green, began to flash red. Like a car stuck with its hazards on, they clicked on and off at an even tempo.

And continued to do so.

Julian punched the air clumsily, like a prizefighter in a gas leak. He bounced back into the car, whacked the roof, and yelled '*Next!*' And so, that's what they did. Icehouse's 'We Can Get Together' blared from the car radio, and the young men in the car drunkenly bellowed what lyrics they could remember, in between stopping at every intersection between Manly and the Spit, turning every set of traffic lights to hazard mode for the foreseeable future.

Behind them, the dribble of early morning traffic began to build up, honking crazily when cars coming from the other direction screeched to a halt, each driver assuming the flashing meant some disaster had befallen the area. If you were to coast above this scene, you'd see a sedan driving nightmarishly fast with pinpoint precision, stopping occasionally to futz with the lights at major intersections, before continuing on its way. Traffic was, according to reports Julian showed John the next day, backed up for miles. Bedlam.

Nobody got hurt, though. My morals, thought John to himself, haven't fallen off the wagon. They're just a little loose.

31

THE HAUNTING OF NORTH SYDNEY STATION

The day after their traffic-ruining bender, remarkably underslept and hungover, John and Julian were called to Neutral Bay to deal with a shoplifter at Woolies. The store had in their custody an enormous bearded man with a magnificent blond quiff, who stared down the two police as they entered the staffroom to survey the situation. John sized the guy up. He was about 130 kilograms of pure muscle with a beard in the colour, and size, of a haystack. He was a fucking obelisk. He did, however, play it very cool, and it was a minor shoplifting offence; namely a packet of Juicy Fruit chewing gum, which he'd been caught with on his way out. So John asked if Woolies wanted to press charges – they did not – and they sent him on his way. Afterwards, John and Julian grabbed a quick bite. All in all, not a bad case to deal with on a hangover. Low impact. John prayed he'd dealt with his last dickhead of the shift.

Once they returned to the station, John and Julian found themselves on desk duty. Whether this was because someone had reported them John couldn't be certain, though to be honest, he was glad to be sitting down with ready access to coffee.

By this point, John had introduced Julian to Christine, and off-duty, the three had been socialising with some success – it meant a great deal to John that his new best friend —

Before I can think, a long 'awwww' escapes my mouth. To hear Dad use the phrase 'best friend' is a rare, unconscious reveal. I smile apologetically. We've never been an 'awwww' household, largely because Dad can't abide an 'awwww', and going on the face he's pulling, he certainly doesn't now.

It meant a great deal to John that his fiancée and his best friend got along. Any concerns John might have had about the two getting along – beyond just pleasantries, outside of work – disappeared that very evening at the end of their shifts. Julian had shuffled back to his desk as John and Christine were chatting nearby.

'Listen,' he began, wringing his hands as if he were in trouble. 'This is going to sound a little fucked, but I need help with something.' From there, John and Christine sat back and heard his predicament.

Julian, it transpired, had an ex who'd gone a bit wobbly. Christine pressed him for more details, and in a roundabout way, unaccustomed as he was to making intimate confessions of a personal nature, Julian detailed their messy breakup. He talked through how she seemed to take it well initially, until the phone calls started. Then she started showing up at his house, making a scene, crying outside his window. He then explained the reason he needed their help now was that she'd abandoned this stratagem, and that she'd now taken to waiting for him outside the station each shift and was refusing to leave his side until he took her back. John didn't know any of this, and was just as lost as Julian. He had no idea what he could do to help.

Christine, however, wasn't as lost in this arena. She got straight to the point and told Julian that he needed to tell his ex to leave him alone. Julian said he'd done that, several times. She suggested a restraining order. He said he just needed to avoid her for as long as he could and she'd calm down. Christine thought about that for a second, then said, 'Come with me.'

Five minutes later, Christine was driving past Julian's ex, perched across the street waiting on a bench, eyeing the exit to the station hungrily. Christine drove around the corner to Julian's parked car, stopped, and coolly walked around to the boot. She popped it open, and after a moment, out crawled Julian. He looked around furtively to make sure he was in the clear, leapt out, then straightened his hair and laughed. Christine laughed back, sighed, and minutes later was back at John's desk relaying the entire story.

'Anyway, gotta head off. See you after work,' she said, touching his hand and trotting away.

His shift after that turned into something of a by-the-numbers slog. By 10 p.m., things had got oddly quiet. John had got up to use the toilet, when he heard a strange crying and banging noise coming from the cells. Puzzled, he looked around to see if anyone else had noticed. Richie sat across the room, doing paperwork, oblivious. Evidently John was the only one.

He decided to stretch his legs and head down to the cell area to check on things. Scanning the chart by the door, he saw that only one person was in the tank: a drunk in his twenties. John toddled down the corridor, opened the slot in the door and looked in. The frantic young man inside looked genuinely rattled, and ran towards the door, his eyes wide.

'Fuck. Shit. Um . . . Hi. Can I change cells, please? I don't like it in here.'

John took a tiny step backwards. 'That's . . . not really a thing we do. Do you need some water? I can get you some water.'

The man looked exasperated. He shook his head, took a deep breath and tried again. Only this time he threw a curveball John was ill prepared for.

'It's haunted.'

This was an interesting development.

'Haunted?'

'Yes! Yes. Yes it's haunted. Shit. I don't like it here. Please move me somewhere else.'

The man, only now realising how insane he sounded, looked around and lowered his voice to a whisper.

'Um . . . Someone is talking to me from inside the walls.'

John explained to the man that he was the only person in the cell block that night, and when the man insisted this be confirmed, John decided to go through the motions and check anyway, like a parent placating a kid who was convinced there was a gorgon waiting to pounce under their bed. First the cell to the left, then the cell to the right . . . nobody. The guy was clearly very drunk, but maybe he was very high, too. Or very sick in the head.

John told the man to wait – a prospect which almost sent the guy into shock – and headed out to see if anyone could help him out. Richie had gone, but thankfully, he spotted Dunne. After listening patiently to what John relayed, Dunne nodded and grabbed the keys.

'No point letting the feller shit himself on account of us being sticklers, mate. Come on,' he said, smiling as he led John back down to the cells. Dunne opened the cell door, and moved the man to another cell right down at the other end of the corridor. The man was almost jumping out of his skin with gratitude, going to shake Dunne's hand before opting instead to pat his arm awkwardly, and voluntarily leapt into his new cell without any prompting at all.

John thanked Dunne and headed back to his desk. After twenty minutes or so of plodding away on his paperwork, a constable John had seen around once or twice, McKenzie, sat down opposite him with a cup of tea. McKenzie smiled and nodded at John. He was about forty, bald, and had a goatee. He had tiny, twinkling eyes. John noticed he was missing the end of his thumb. McKenzie saw him staring.

'Got caught in a door. Fucking hurt, too.' He smiled, cutting John off. 'S'okay. I'd look, too.' After a moment, John decided he needed to run this 'haunted cell' nonsense by someone else, so he cleared his throat and told McKenzie the entire thing. When he'd finished, McKenzie threw him a strange look. 'Hang on. What cell was that?'

John peered back down the corridor to check. 'Uhh . . . cell four.'

McKenzie looked coldly at John, all sparkle gone from his eyes. He rubbed his jaw, looking troubled. After a long pause, he spoke.

'Cell four *is* haunted, mate. People hear voices in there all the time, have since . . . Shit, five years, at *least*. I've had to move three people out of there. Always happens around this time of night, too.'

John laughed, thinking here it was: third dickhead of the night. His laugh died off. McKenzie wasn't laughing. He got up to leave then turned to John one last time.

'I should put a sign on the door or something.'

He walked off towards the bathrooms.

John thought back to the kid at Luna Park, and was suddenly aware of how old and still the building was. As subtly as he could, he got up and changed desks so he wasn't looking directly down at the cell blocks.

32

BACK TO SCHOOL

Time passed uneventfully over the ensuing weeks. John, Julian and Richie grew closer – often with the aid of copious quantities of alcohol – and John and Christine discussed wedding plans. Her transfer finally came through – a job in police recruitment at head office, and before he knew it, John had to head back to the academy to finally break free of probation. This meant six more weeks back in secondary training for his last stint at the academy.

John and Julian had been dreading this return to school. It felt like a demotion; Julian in particular recoiled at the idea of giving back his badge and gun and sitting in a classroom, and as the date approached, he got more and more agitated. Swearier. He was cursing like a sailor, and had taken to walking in tiny circles and muttering angrily to himself.

John wasn't looking forward to it, either, but he had another problem. John had actually cashed in his annual leave to go on the trip to Fiji with Christine. Not that he'd change any of that period (apart from perhaps the shitting mother incident) in a million years. But it did mean that his time back at the mammoth installation was, frankly, isolating, and depressing as hell. Only two things of note happened during this period.

> 'Paul . . . I might need to run you through this first thing a little . . . tentatively. So you're aware of Roger Rogerson, aren't you?'
>
> He has my full attention now. I know that Dad was involved in some dicey shit – or was at least witness to it – but at no point did I think it would be connected to Roger Rogerson, the most infamous of New South Wales detectives Rogerson sits at the core of the most scandalous, infamous and horrifying instalment of New South Wales police history, and I never thought we'd be discussing it. Dad notices that I'm firing on all cylinders, and gestures for me to settle down and listen.
>
> 'Right. So the word in the media at the time was that Warren Lanfranchi, the drug dealer who Rogerson shot, had . . . well, was armed. But the word in the inner sanctum, on the QT . . . let me wind back a bit.'

John had been back on secondary training for a few days, and had just finished a slew of physical tests. He'd headed into the bathroom area to shower, shit and shave. A room with rows of lockers and benches led into a large communal prison-style shower. John had just entered and was getting undressed when he heard voices behind some lockers. Three or four young men were speaking in hushed tones.

Out of little more than idle curiosity, John hung back to eavesdrop. He'd somehow placed himself in an area between the three young men and the door, so he knew at some point he'd have to say hi. For now, though, he went with his inquisitive instincts and listened in.

He recognised one of the voices: a friendly cadet named Ben whom he'd chatted with in this very locker room twice since coming back. Ben was a probationary constable who, like John, had been out in the field for a number of months. He was in his early twenties, was bald, and was built for running through walls, but he was nice enough. And his friends were grilling him on Lanfranchi. It was all anyone was talking about at the time, so initially John thought nothing of it. He listened as they ran through the same details he'd heard over and over already.

Warren Lanfranchi, a low-rent criminal piece of shit, was on the way to a robbery in North Sydney, and he was hiding down by the back seat of a car being driven by two other crims. The car came off the ramp up towards North Sydney station, and a highway patrol motorcyclist pulled the car over for a traffic matter, not sure what. But he didn't know – obviously – that Lanfranchi was lying in wait in the back with a sawn-off rifle trained on him. Ben was getting more and more hushed as the story progressed; his friends listened with rapt attention. John strained his ears to keep up, and flattened himself against the cold lockers.

The gun, explained Ben, didn't work properly. Misfired. 'The pin didn't come down on the bullet, who knows?' he whispered. 'Either way, the cop sees this, they lose their shit and they piss off in the car. Warren was a scumbag, but he was protected by Roger Rogerson. Rogerson may have used him for various things, called in favours, I'm not clear on the specifics.'

There was a pause. It had gone quiet; John thought for an agonising stretch that he'd been caught eavesdropping. He briefly considered sneaking out, but he'd heard the magic words. Roger Rogerson.

Then Ben continued, measuring every word. 'Here's the thing, though – I was on probation with a partner of Rogerson's. And I was there when the two of them were talking one night, they obviously didn't think I was nearby listening in —' *The irony*, John thought, tensing every muscle in his body '— and Rogerson said he'd decided trying to shoot a police officer was crossing the line. Said it was "personal". So these two organised to meet Lanfranchi in an alleyway, and shot him. I heard the call later on, confirming it had gone down. It was fucked. It was . . . it was fucked.'

The story was over, and John had moments to come up with a story of his own as to why he was sitting perched behind a wall of lockers, clearly listening in on a very dangerous piece of inside information. He heard the three young men standing up to leave and quickly did the first thing that occurred to him.

He crouched down holding his towel in place, and slid underneath the row of benches. Three pairs of feet padded past, and off outside. Once he was certain they were gone, he crawled out and swore to himself. That was too close.

Not long after that, John was at the city morgue doing some routine work, and the pathologist, who'd taken a liking to him during probation, gave him a mysterious look and stopped him briefly outside a small, dark room. 'Won't believe who we've got in there,' he said. 'Warren Lanfranchi.' He looked like a cool uncle who was about to let his nephew ride his Harley while the parents weren't watching. And remembering the information he'd purloined in a state of semi-undress not long before, John didn't miss a beat and immediately took a swing, asking if he could have a quick look. The pathologist shrugged, nodded, and swung open the door.

There was Warren Lanfranchi, naked, on the slab. John noted the entry wound on his forehead, one to the side of his head, and one in the chest. But what really drew the eye was what the late Lanfranchi was doing with his right hand.

John knew Rogerson was a detective, and he still harboured a kind of romanticised ideal of being one. But he was fast figuring out what types of people can end up working as detectives. John considered this fact as he stared at what lay in front of him.

The dead hand of Lanfranchi was wrapped firmly around the dead penis of Lanfranchi.

After he was shot – but before he'd, well, stiffened – someone had carefully wrapped his hand around his dick. A clear as day fuck-you to the guy. Very, very personal. Safe bet, John thought to himself, it was the same guy who shot him.

A guy who thought it was personal.

John had been hanging out with Julian and Richie several times a week, and their friendships continued to grow. In the interim he'd also moved in with Christine, and they'd had a quick, cheap, but warm wedding. But before long, the thing consuming his every waking thought was exams. Getting back on the job. He was finally nearing the end of secondary and was sitting in a sprawling exam room, head down, frantically scribbling down answers to such police obscura as 'is it an offence for a horse to defecate in public?' *Yes*, he wrote. *Yes it is*. His time away from the job he loved, harrowing as it was, would draw to a close once he had officially broken free of academy life.

It was early afternoon, and all two hundred people in the exam room were reaching a fever pitch of nerves and exhaustion, when a senior officer walked over to John, leaned down, and whispered, 'Probationary Constable Verhoeven? Phone call for you. Urgent. Outside.' John, relieved to escape the exam but now nervous about the content of the phone call, stood up and made his way towards the exit. Eyes followed him as he went.

He snatched up the phone and said hello.

'This is recruiting, calling for Probationary Constable John Verhoeven?'

Even putting on her best crisp, stern work voice, he could tell it was Christine. He wilted, grinning like an idiot. 'How's the exam going?' she asked. He began to tell her. She cut him off.

'I'm pregnant!'

There was a lengthy and appropriately pregnant pause. John didn't know this, but he had a throaty little 'hoooo!' noise he made when he was excited. Under his breath, without realising it, he did so now. Christine knew how he felt.

After a precious minute of chatter, he told her he loved her, and ran back into the exam room to conclude his work. On checking the clock on the wall he saw he had another full hour of questions to answer about the legality of leaving horse shit on a public footpath in contravention of various laws.

He could have floated out the window right then and there.

33

CUT TO THE CHASE

Christine was pregnant but still several months away from being unceremoniously told that any leave she took to have kids would seriously harm her career. And John was now back at work, back at North Sydney with Julian and Richie. As luck would have it, John's first shift back was with Julian. A day shift. John almost hugged Julian when he jogged up to the car before they set out.

> Dad takes a sip of water and gives me this look. A very kind look. And, unbidden, he makes a sudden overt concession to all my nerd stuff.
> 'It was like when Spock yelled *JIM!*, Paul.'
> He gives me a *how'd-I-do?* look. I tell him I couldn't be prouder.

They clapped each other on the back and got into their car. They'd been driving along for ten minutes or so when John dropped the bombshell.

'So . . . we're having a baby.'

Julian hit the brakes, momentarily swerving into traffic. He whooped like a maniac, eyes lit up, and laughed in John's face. '*Yes!* We're having a baby! That's . . . oh, John. Mate. You and I are going to make *wonderful* parents.'

John punched Julian in the arm. 'John, shit. That's great. It's very quick, but you do tend to go a bit quick with this stuff. Congratulations, mate. Fucking beautiful news.'

Julian ruffled John's hair and whooped again. John couldn't have imagined a warmer response. He let this sink in for a while. He'd just had an idea but wanted to let it cook a little. Julian was right, after all: he did move a little quick sometimes.

The following week, John found himself working a shift out of the Mosman station, once again with Julian. They'd been sent to run an errand out of area, and were cruising along from North Sydney to Manly. The window was down, and they were chatting happily.

'See, by this point,' Dad says, 'we had a bit of a reputation.'

'For messing with traffic lights?'

'Yes. But also for working well together as a team. Julian and I had a lot in common in terms of police work, but we also liked the same films, the same music. You know how young men in their twenties are – they like to jam their tastes down other people's throats, surround themselves with people who like exactly what they do. I didn't have too many mates in the force, but Julian and I agreed on just about everything. So we'd swap vinyl – I was *obsessed* with Jean Luc Ponty, Tangerine Dream, Kraftwerk, Talking Heads, Frank Zappa.'

Suddenly, it dawns on me. 'Dad! You were a hipster!'

Dad looks at me like I've just slapped his drink out of his hand. 'What?'

'You were a fucking hipster! Obscure vinyl? Ironically reading shit like *The Thorn Birds*?'

Dad looks offended, and one of his eyelids flutters, like he's suppressing a small rage-induced stroke. 'I didn't do anything ironically, Paul. And I'm going to pretend you didn't say that. The point is, Julian and I had a lot in common, which actually helped when it came to police work. Because we saw eye to eye on the little things, and by extension, the big things too. And even with the detectives yanking Cardigan out from under us, we still had an impressive arrest record. See, we actually went out and looked for arrests. We *wanted* to work. Which meant that by the time we got back from secondary, certain people higher up were watching us keenly. And we got wind of this, so we got a bit . . . jumpy. Either we were up for a promotion, or we were treading on toes.'

John and Julian were heading to Manly when, out from a busy lane of traffic, a silver Ford Falcon burst away, swerved onto the wrong side of the road, and began to accelerate pell-mell in a huge, smoky arc. All in clear view of the patrol car. And given their eagerness to galvanise their slowly growing reputation as go-getters, they nodded at each other with the unspoken language of any two people who understand each other, flipped on the light, hit the siren and gave pursuit.

The car, drifting dangerously and fishtailing slightly from side to side, burned up Sydney Road. John looked at the speedo, 140 kilometres per hour and Julian's feet hadn't touched the brakes in a full minute. John could feel himself being pushed back into his seat, and he had a flashback to being pinned to the seat in Woodstock's patrol car a year earlier, chasing a scared man down an alley. He had zero idea what the guy in the Falcon had done to spur him into driving that fast away from cops. Every moment that passed in their chase, John was tallying up new charges – reckless driving, reckless endangerment, property damage. As if on cue, the car sheared the side mirror off a parked hatchback and pulled a clean ninety-degree turn down towards the Spit Bridge. Julian followed suit. John could feel his last meal lurching nastily to one side in his stomach.

By the time they crossed the bridge, they had yet to stop or slow down. Their patrol car swooped towards the tiny gap between the toll booths and Julian whooped as seconds ahead of them, the Falcon struck the yellow and black arm of the gate, which detonated instantly in a shower of splinters. John glanced at the speedometer again: 160 kilometres per hour. As they passed the booth, he made eye contact with the elderly attendant inside, and they zipped through with such force there was a faint, deep noise like a cork leaving its bottle. With a shuddering pop and skid of tyres, Julian weaved their car down the off-ramp, his knuckles stark white against the black of the wheel.

John had been radioing for assistance for five full minutes, but because of the speeds at which they were passing through different police areas VKG had opened the frequency to any and all cars who could get to them. This meant that by the time they were passing through Taylor Square, Julian was almost driven off the road by a small fleet of paddy wagons. Some were from Mosman, one was from Neutral Bay and three were from the city. One of the drivers yelled something at John and made some hand gestures. John nodded and mouthed 'OK'.

'What are they saying?' Julian yelled over the siren.

John shrugged. 'I think they want us to pull back.'

And so that's what they did. Gradually, they eased off, and in an instant, like some kind of horrifying steel catcher's mitt, the mass of wagons surrounded and enveloped the Falcon. If the goal of a car chase is to push someone past their limits and make them crash, this was a masterful display; as one, like a flock of birds, the wagons sped up and tried to pull up and over the embankment. The Falcon, having nowhere to go, fucked up the manoeuvre and one of its wheel arches burst. It began to grind to a halt, and the wagons kept their formation. Julian slowed to a stop next to the grid of vehicles, and they watched, fascinated, as the car they'd been chasing across the city came to a stop.

John turned the siren off.

Typically at this point they'd have hopped out of the car, traipsed over and arrested the guy, which would have meant considerable paperwork back at the station. This course of action turned out to be moot, however, as they watched one of the officers jump from his wagon onto the hood of the Falcon, smash the windscreen with his baton, wrench the driver out by the scruff of his neck, drag him over to the nearest wagon and hurl him in the back like he was a pile of dirty laundry. The officer then turned to John and Julian, and with a big smile on his face, gave them a tiny golf clap. Two of the other officers, still inside their wagons, joined in. John and Julian, tickled and confused, but glad to have gotten, if nothing else, the thrill of a paperwork-free car chase out of the proceedings returned the clap.

Chuffed at their freebie, a rare treat, they let their adrenaline settle back down and slowly began to cross back over into the city. They were halfway across the Harbour Bridge when out of nowhere, the impossible happened. Lightning struck twice. A red Holden Monaro overtook them doing 100 kilometres per hour in the 60 lane. Four men were inside. Just like that, it was back on.

Julian gave chase, and as he worked his way up to full speed their car was almost clipped by a stream of five other patrol cars, all going after the same guys.

So John and Julian happily joined in. It was a warm night, so John wound down his window and smiled. He knew this was a strange way to unwind, but he was having a wonderful time.

Eventually, they arrived at the site where the chase had ended. They rounded the corner down on Willoughby Road, near the old Channel 9 studios, and it was utter bedlam. The Monaro had pulled up – well crashed, really. Patrol cars were arriving and parking, and cops were running around like maniacs barking orders, looking for the occupants of the car, who'd clearly fucked off somewhere. So Julian pulled up and they sat there, the two of them surveying the scene. Cops were trying to get into the buildings nearby, yelling into radios and generally running around like headless chooks.

That's when John spotted an apartment block on the other side of the road, right near where they were sitting, complete with a ramp heading down to an underground car park. There was nowhere else the suspects could have gone, and not a single cop was looking down there, or was anywhere near there. John tapped Julian on the shoulder and beckoned with his index finger. Julian nodded.

They coolly hopped out, kept their heads down and strolled over to the underground car park. Miraculously, the gate was raised. They squinted in the shitty lighting. It was very quiet, and every noise John and Julian made echoed crazily. A smattering of parked vehicles stretched back thirty metres or so, dull grey pillars punctuating the darkness. And after a minute or so of looking under cars, John heard something. So did Julian, as a matter of fact.

A sneeze.

The noise echoed through the cavernous space, shortly followed by someone muttering 'shit'.

A minute later, Julian and John walked back up the steep entrance to the car park with the four men from the Monaro, cuffed and trudging in front of them into the arms of the waiting throng of cops. There were no golf claps this time, just proper handshakes and well dones, and congratulations.

John and Julian had been back in the saddle a week, and already they'd taken their reputation up another level.

34

BETTER NOT WRIST IT

Christine was set on the idea of having the baby at the Royal North Shore Hospital. She'd made some calls, and some friends who'd had their kids there had sold her on it. John, on the other hand, became oddly fixated on, in that uniquely male way, the idea that he knew what was best. He was born at Mater Hospital in Crows Nest, so that's where he wanted his kid to be born. 'Mater Hospital, Christine,' he insisted over the phone. It's absurd that this was the topic where he put his foot down for the first time in this relationship, but that's how it goes sometimes. He was feeling stubborn and he held his ground. They say pick your battles; perhaps the adage should be amended to 'pick your battles and don't be a dickhead'.

'We'll talk about this another time,' she said, but it was clear the roller doors had come down. End of conversation. He'd fucked up. 'I love you,' he ventured. 'Mhmm,' came her reply, and she hung up. It was their first fight.

John was station constable for his shift, and his boss for the day was Joe Harding. John liked Harding. He was greying, in his late fifties, and never left the confines of the station to go on patrol, or much of anything else. If it was possible to haunt a building, but to do so in a good way and to be respected by all and sundry, that was Joe: a helpful geist. He was unflappable, cool as a cucumber – provided that cucumber was stored at the recommended temperature. Charlie Manson could have been slavering away in front of him for an hour straight and Joe wouldn't have broken a sweat. And Joe Harding liked John. He liked John just fine.

Which suited John on this particular day. Nothing helped him get a handle on stress like the gratifying monotony of station duties. Their rhythmic monotony took him out of himself. Answering the Sylvester switch, sorting out prisoners' meals, photographing, fingerprinting, telegraphing, message book, dispatches, telexes . . . it was overwhelming at times, but it took you out of your head and made the time fly by.

At about eleven that morning, the doors were tossed open. Highway patrol dragged in a man well over two metres tall, pupils fully dilated, ranting insanely. His sandy blond locks were matted, and drool shone on his chin and soaked his shirt. He locked eyes with John. John wondered if Manson would, in fact, give this guy a run for his money.

The man was nineteen and high on LSD. He was foaming at the mouth as the highway patrolmen relayed this information to the predictably unperturbed Harding, who sat there, implacable, taking notes in his tiny, neat handwriting. The prisoner made sickening wheezing noises and strained to get away, as a vein the length of the Marianas Trench pulsed rhythmically on his forehead. Sweat and spit occasionally flew through the air, catching the light and landing on an expressionless Harding, who calmly wiped his glasses and continued to nod and take notes.

What John overheard next had him drop any pretence of being hard at work and he leaned forward, rapt.

The two highway patrolmen had been driving along a side street several suburbs away when, out of the blue – or to be accurate, the bushes nearby – a trail bike bearing one slavering maniac with whom John was now tangentially acquainted had crested the rise, soared through the air and collided with the side of the patrol car. From there, the maniac had tumbled over the car and flipped head over arse into a different set of bushes, where he lay until he was bundled into the car which he'd collided with and whisked to the station.

Joe, as if sensing John's willingness to become a part of this wretched tale, turned to John for help in putting the prisoner into a cell. The prisoner, gurning loudly and grinding his teeth, locked eyes with John. John stared right back. The prisoner barked like a dog.

All right, thought John. Let's get this over with.

He led the man, whose name turned out to be Arthur, back and into a special cell. Most cells at the station had barred doors, but this cell was older. Its door was massive, thick and heavy, and only interrupted by a handle on its exterior, and a semicircular metal flap for those officers brave enough to slide food through. John bundled Arthur inside, and he promptly struck up a conversation with an obliging wall. John shut the door, sighed, and headed back to his desk. His sweet, sweet desk, where the sketchiest thing he'd encounter would be a paper cut.

After half an hour, Joe turned to John. 'John, do me a favour? Head down to the Greasy Spoon, get him a coffee and a sandwich. There's a good lad.'

John, always keen for an excuse to stretch his legs, headed across the road and into the Greasy Spoon, and then ferried his revolting but technically edible coffee-and-sandwich cargo towards the cell.

He knocked, pulled down the flap and practically flung the food in before scampering off. Job done.

That is, until an hour later when Harding turned to John again. 'John, mate . . . Bit quiet back there. Go check on our guest, if you'd be so kind.' He said this while looking over his glasses like a kindly old librarian. John couldn't refuse so he stood and made his way down to the now oddly quiet cell block.

He listened for something, anything, as he approached the door. Dead silence. With a slow, careful motion, John reached out, unlatched the flap and lowered it.

Across the cell, next to the far wall and talking to himself, was the prisoner. His wrists had been hacked open, and his hands were covered in blood. On the floor below lay the uneaten sandwich, the styrofoam cup, and . . . the plastic lid, folded in half, covered in blood and skin. The prisoner looked up at John with a quick snap of his head, eyes like two black buttons sewn on, and made a cheerful 'wheeeee!' sound. John swore.

John eventually convinced the gibbering man to thrust his ruined wrists through the flap. He stood in the corridor, listening to the prisoner muttering to himself indistinctly about how he had 'things hidden inside him' and that he 'needed to get them out', and dabbed disinfectant on the wounds. He discovered as he worked that the damage looked much worse than it actually was. After cleaning them as best he could, he set to bandaging the gnawed wrists. Once he'd done that John gave the man's hands an awkward pat. A feeble 'there you go, in you pop' pat, the kind his mother gave him when he'd skinned his knee. The hands slid back silently into the recess, the man who owned them gave a strange belch and a popping noise, and John gladly slammed the flap shut. That, as they say, was that.

Another half-hour passed, and John found himself forgetting

about the prisoner, about the wrists, about the coffee cup. He began processing paperwork and losing himself in the drudgery. And because the universe sometimes takes moments like this to really fuck with you, because lightning does sometimes strike twice, Harding soon waved at John again.

'John! Bit quiet, mate. Best go check again. Give us a yell if . . . you know.'

John nodded, suppressed a sigh, and stood up. Moments later he was winding his way down the corridor yet again. It was, as Harding had noted, quiet.

Too quiet.

John extended his hand yet again, winced, and opened the flap. And . . .

Nobody was inside.

Whatever bleary-eyed paperwork torpor John had been resting in shattered, and he snapped into action. He checked again. No prisoner. The cell was empty. But . . . how? How could a man who'd lost blood and was out of his brain on hallucinogens have escaped from a bolted and secure century-old cell?

Without warning, the prisoner appeared, his face pressed against the opening, his tongue lolling. He screamed, made a high-pitched braying sound and stood back, raising his wrists to proudly display his handiwork.

The man's face was slick with blood, his teeth were clogged with skin and hair, gristle and sinew. John fought to keep his lunch down as he took in what Arthur was so clearly proud of: he'd ripped the bandages away with his teeth, then continued on, taking huge, ragged bites out of his wrists. Tendons were exposed and black, viscous blood eked out in slow gouts. He'd eaten his way right down to the bone.

Arthur fixed John with a look that bored through him, and in a calm voice, intoned:

'I didn't feel like a sandwich.'

John screamed – yelped, really – and ran, slipping over on the way to Harding's desk.

The ambulance officers rushed in as John was clocking off for the day, Harding having taken pity on him and told him to head home after making a quick official report on the whole incident. John, still shaking, made for his apartment.

Well . . . *their* apartment. As he entered, he saw Christine, sitting there smiling up at him. And he remembered the fight from the morning, and he remembered how difficult he'd been. But because he was tired, he decided not to talk about it. He resolved to deal with it later. It would simply be too harrowing in his current state. Not 'chew through your wrists because the Greasy Spoon is inedible' harrowing, but harrowing nonetheless.

Not twenty minutes had passed when, curled up on the couch with his arm around Christine, sleep beginning to overtake him, the local news caught his eye. A live feed snapped across to a dapper looking middle-aged reporter, clutching a microphone and eyes locked onto the camera.

'I'm here in Crows Nest, Sydney, where a situation is developing!' the man barked over the sound of a helicopter. John watched, rapt and terrified, as a spotlight swung through the shot and up the building. The camera followed, zooming and focusing as best it could until it came to rest on the distant roof of the hospital. There, a man with wild blond hair and bandaged wrists could be seen hanging from a precarious drainpipe. As the camera zoomed in closer, John could see that he was ranting inaudibly at the nearby helicopter. And right next to him, lit up and clear as day, was the hospital sign.

Mater Hospital.

'You know what?' said John, turning to Christine slowly. 'Let's go with the Royal North Shore.'

35

HOW TO SUCCEED IN HITCHHIKING WITHOUT REALLY TRYING

John and Julian were on the up and up. Even Dunne had thrown John the odd passing remark – 'You're going to make the rest of us lads look bad, you are' – and he noticed that he and Julian were getting rostered on together more and more. Which was when he and Julian hit upon a novel but not entirely new idea.

Fishing.

Here's how John and Julian went fishing. First, they began a shift by moving their car into particularly dense traffic. This, in John's mind, was like nestling your hook right in the middle of a school of fish. (Actually, John was terrible at proper fishing, hence the flimsiness of this metaphor.) Then, they flashed their light and waited to see if anyone bolted. Most times it didn't work, though if he listened very carefully, he could hear the anuses of everyone within spitting distance snap shut, like fifty airlocks sucking closed in unison.

One Thursday night, however, they were in traffic close to the station when Julian made the call and threw out the line. He flashed the light and —

WHAM!

A sudden roar of rubber and metal as a white Falcon 500 flew past them. They'd landed a big one, too. For a brief moment John saw a bearded, heavily tattooed man in the driver's seat, angrily gunning it down the road. They gave chase.

As they reached Mosman, the Falcon began to do what many wily criminals do: it attempted to burrow into side street after side street to try to throw John and Julian off its tail. Julian had no problem keeping up. But John, who was calling the chase down the radio street by street to keep the station apprised of their location, began to struggle. One of the quirks of Mosman's streets is that after a time they stop having names and start having numbers, prefixed by the letter 'M'. With his head spinning from endless hard turns and motion sickness crawling up his throat to nest behind his eyes, John had to concede he was utterly lost. He couldn't tell where they were on these minor streets, and there was a distinct lack of streetlights to help him. The only thing illuminated was the car in front of them.

Finally, they were slowing down. 'We've got him! Dead end, mate,' Julian said, popping on the handbrake. John looked around to see where they'd ended up.

They were in a narrow, cobblestoned lane lined with garage roller doors belonging to various homes. At the end of the way he could just make out a grey, mottled wooden fence. Two overstuffed bins sat propped against it. The Falcon idled there, its driver not moving.

This wasn't a good sign. Nine times out of ten, when a car chase ends, the driver, having run his vehicle into the ground, continues his locomotive assholery with a foot chase. 'If someone doesn't run after a chase,' Dunne once told John, 'odds are they're not scared of you.' Right now, John and Julian were helplessly lost. Any backup they were hoping for would have zero idea where they were. And what if Dunne was right? What if this driver wasn't scared *for a reason*? This was bad news. Very bad news.

The slam of a door startled John out of his musings. Julian was halfway to the Falcon, flashlight out, gun drawn. John swore under his breath, pulled his gun and hopped out too.

A lot of things happened very quickly at this point.

Firstly, as Julian's flashlight beam filled the cabin of the Falcon, John saw there were two people inside, not one. The passenger seat was occupied by a long-haired, bearded young man. Julian, clearly baffled as to how he could have missed such a detail, threw the door open, wrenched the young man out and slung him up against a roller door. The loud *pang!* sound filled the alleyway, and the man promptly shat himself.

Secondly, the now shit-stained man began screaming, 'I'm a hitchhiker! I'm a hitchhiker! I'm a fucking hitchhiker, man, I'm sorry!'

Julian scanned the quivering mess, registered the backpack on his back, and his face softened. 'All right, go on, get out of here. Any problems, call North Sydney police station, they'll sort you out.' The young man ran as fast as he could, streaming 'thankyou thankyou thankyou' into the night.

Thirdly, John remembered his light and shone it on the driver. The driver who hadn't moved this entire time, and was slyly smiling to himself. As John's torch swung downwards, the man's hand began creeping towards his glovebox. 'Hands where I can see them!' John barked, pointing his gun into the open window of the driver's side. He opened the door, pulled the man out, and handed him over to Julian. A second, louder *Pang!* echoed through the dark alleyway. The man said nothing, but kept smiling.

Finally, as Julian read the driver his rights, John decided it was time to check the glovebox. He knelt down, propping the car door open with one knee, and gingerly pulled the handle. The glovebox sprang open, and out spilled . . .

Ninja stars.

And they weren't toy ones, either. John touched the tip of one, and drew blood. He looked further into the glovebox. There were several knives of various lengths and a sinister-looking half-used roll of gaffer tape. Behind that, surgical gloves, and a bundle of tools for doing break-and-enters. John stood bolt upright, shut the car door and told Julian to cuff the guy, adding, 'And don't let him out of your sight.'

Julian nodded, and John, knowing they were way out of their depth, listened for sirens. They were close, but there was no way in hell the backup would find them here. He made a snap decision, and bolted towards the entrance to the lane, leaving Julian alone with a man the size of the Incredible Hulk.

Somehow, miraculously, John flagged down a nearby patrol car that had taken a swing and begun to head further into the backstreets, and half an hour later, they were back at the station. John and Julian were knee-deep in paperwork when a pair of detectives trailed out of the interrogation room where The Hulk was being questioned. One of them peeled off and approached their desk.

'Right, so we've questioned him. Nice work there. Very nice work.'

Julian perked up, looking flattered. John, still fostering a beef after their jewellery shafting, simply raised an eyebrow. The detective, sensing the hostility, just shrugged.

'Anyway, thought you might like to know he was wanted for a string of B&Es, and a few sexual assaults. Oh, and a year ago he escaped from prison over in Canberra, was in the wind well before pulling this shit.'

John's eyes widened.

The detective smiled.

'Oh, and he said to say that we should tell the hitchhiker he's sorry for all the fuss and he hopes he got home OK. You two know anything about a hitchhiker?'

John and Julian shook their heads in unison.

Good partners, after all, think the same.

36

TRACK WORK

'So I'm going to be born pretty soon, I'm guessing. Were you looking forward to being a dad?'

My question takes Dad by surprise. He sits up, clearly shaken out of reliving a string of cases involving high-fives with Julian and jubilant car chases. I think he expects me to follow up with a joke. When I don't, he does that lovely thing that Dad does whenever I blindside him with a serious question.

He mulls it over.

See, Dad and I rarely . . . think. Our thoughts tend to coalesce as we say them, which means we often say catastrophically dumb shit, but that dumb shit always comes from a good place. So the fact that Dad is sitting there and trying to answer a serious question shows how earnestly he's taking this entire thing.

He rolls my question around his head for a minute.

'Yeah,' he says.

Another pause. 'That's it? Yeah?'

'No, dickhead, that's not it. I was just thinking of how to frame this next story.' He rubs his eyes and leans back. 'Right.

So Christine is getting big by this point. Jules and I were making a name for ourselves, and one night, still on general duties, I'm rostered on with this young guy. Kevo. And we get a call as the sun is setting to head down to the railway tracks a couple of hundred metres outside St Leonards station.'

John and Kevo pulled down Christie Street, slowly heading towards a group of rail workers flagging them down. The headlights caught their high-vis vests, and they signalled and pointed into the darkness where the tracks lay. John nodded, and his partner steered the car past the assembled group, before finding a spot to park. John hopped out and sent Kevo to go talk to the workers and get a read on the situation, before he walked over towards the tracks.

They'd not been briefed on what was about to happen, or what *had* happened, rather. John cast his eyes over the six-car passenger train, packed to the gills, sitting in the encroaching darkness, utterly motionless. He looked back over his shoulder. Sure enough, the city train was only several hundred metres short of having made it to St Leonards station. He could see tiny people in the distance, milling about on the platform. He looked back at the train. And rather than seeing a roiling mass of angry businessmen, what he saw was . . .

Shock. People in shock. Never good.

John looked for a way over the fence, and saw a gently rising grassy embankment, which he climbed. He vaulted the fence and landed on the blanket of pebbles that flanked the tracks like bubble wrap, and looked over at the train-driver's car. The driver looked back at him, pale and catatonic, nothing behind the eyes.

He was standing in place, swaying slightly, wringing his hands. For a brief moment he registered the presence of John, this young, skinny cop standing out in the darkness looking up at him. Just for a second, though.

John looked down the length of the train car and began walking, looking for what had caused this train, full to bursting, to stop just shy of its designated stop. He fumbled for his torch, found the button, depressed it, swinging the beam out and over the tracks and the wheels of the train.

It came to rest on a pair of legs.

Lying by the smooth, sheer wheel of the train, toes pointing towards him, feet slack. Female, John thought, shock beginning to set in. He felt all the blood rush from him as he tracked the legs from the feet, up to the backs of the knees, up to two buttocks, which sat flush against the wheel. There was no blood, but they were scuffed and dirty, coated in the same dust which now lay upon John's shoes. He swallowed hard and listened.

And then he heard the voice, coming from underneath the train.

John felt sick, and sad. And lonely. The commuters huddled against the windows and doors all looked down at him, mute, confused, as if they'd heard the voice too and didn't want to drown it out. He looked back – no sign of his partner, who was clearly finding out exactly what happened from the railway workers back where he'd parked. Fuck it, thought John, and he did the only thing he could think of doing – he crawled under the train.

It's peak hour, thought John, and at any moment another train will come steaming up behind this one and reduce me to a smear on the tracks. Any moment now.

It was hot, and the air tasted like sparklers, like hot copper. His torch caught thick, fat swirling particles of dirt. And then, after he'd crawled several metres, he saw the girl.

She was in her early twenties, and had blazing-red, curly hair. Her waist lay flat against the inside of the wheel, which was covered with fine, bloody scratch marks where her hands were uselessly pawing, as if some part of her still fought to free herself from this predicament. John closed his hand gently around her wrist and she stopped scratching. Her hand went still, and he laid it on her stomach.

He looked down. The heat and speed of the wheel had apparently sheared her clean in two, then cauterised the wound. John noted she'd come away partially from the wheel and her intestines had, at some point during her struggles, streamed out of her bottom half like the insides of a piñata, and had heaped themselves next to her in a surprisingly orderly pile. Somehow the train had spun her, sawn her in half, and cast off her clothes. She lay there, naked, her entrails piled on the tracks next to her. The whole thing looked so neat, and so polite. John slowly drew his hand away from them, and looked up at her face, crying silently.

The top of her skull was gone, exposing her brain. John saw that the whites of her eyes had gone a terrible, dark red. He thought back to the bodies he saw on his first day at the morgue, and reminded himself that this was all just stuff. Just matter. He heard the air swirling around them in the hollow space underneath the train, and tried to remember the sound from inside that hollow torso in which he'd been hit with the realisation that death is a real thing, and that he was going to have to deal with it.

She was still talking. Quietly, at first. 'Get it off me. Help me. Help. Get it off,' she muttered. And John held her hand, and told her . . . anything. Just small talk. Meaningless platitudes, the kind of things you tell a kid who just skinned her knee after falling off a bike. 'You're fine, you'll be fine. I'm John, I'm not leaving, OK? Just hang tight, we've got people coming.'

John briefly registered his partner Kevin popping his head under the carriage. He waved him off, then watched as the young man stifled a small retch and got back on his radio before disappearing.

John looked back at the girl.

He took off his police jacket, a nylon number with a thick, furry collar, and draped it over her. She nodded in an empty sort of way, coughed lightly, and started to talk about her father. How much she missed him, how sad he'd be, how he was going to visit soon. She kept trailing off, and began repeating her sentences. Then, after sputtering the word 'Dad' a few times, she started clawing at the wheel once more. John stilled her hand.

He heard sirens from outside. Red and blue lights filled the chamber, and he lay there with her as long as he could before they made him leave.

Twenty minutes later, John was sitting outside with a paramedic, watching as railway rescue workers began the process of trying to move the wheel and get her out. He knew that once the wheel was gone, any life in the girl would flood away, but he wanted to find out who her father was. In railway accidents of this type, with someone pinned to the tracks, their family would typically be called to the site before the removal of what was holding them there.

Emergency services knew, you see, that the removal of the heavy object, or track, or wheel, would kill the person, so they made sure that everyone was there beforehand to say their goodbyes. John looked around vainly. She'd asked for her dad. He wasn't coming.

Two hours later, John was back at the station and was in pretty serious shock, but still he insisted on finishing his paperwork. He looked up as the door opened. An older man came in, hat in hand. John, his mind still reeling and wandering, listened in as the man asked the desk sergeant on duty for help.

He'd travelled down from the country.

His daughter was in an institution, you see.

He was lost, and wanted to know where the institution she was staying at was located.

And she had blazing-red, curly hair.

Dad looks at me, eyes shining.

'I asked Julian to be your godfather the very next day.'

37

DON'T BOTTLE IT UP

Dad and I sit there, sort of traumatised after the train story. Dad has never mentioned this to me before. I've heard of shock syndrome, though. Essentially, the pressure that is killing the person is also holding everything in, holding everything together. Once that pressure is removed, they're free, sure, but toxins flood the body and kill them.

And while telling these stories isn't killing Dad, it is fascinating, and a little sad, watching everything, all these memories that he's never talked about or told openly, come rushing out into the open. I hope I'm not doing any damage making him recount all of these memories. My fundamental objective here is simply to try to process, to come to terms with seeing those fucking horrible photographs as a kid. To try to expunge the gunk it left clinging to my brain, to sort out the recurring nightmares. Then I realise that while I have a photo or two to process, Dad has spent years with the real thing. And far worse. What has that done to him, psychologically?

I hadn't planned on Dad lying with a dying woman as the light went out of her eyes. Dad clears his throat, and his voice wobbles a bit. We share a look in that moment that speaks volumes: he gets that I get it. And he knows we need to change the subject.

'Want to hear a funny story?'

'Yes,' I reply. 'I do.'

Over drinks one night, still months before Christine would give birth, John, Julian and Richie discovered that they were all adept scuba divers. John was surprised it had never come up; they somehow all had their scuba licences, and they all lived on Sydney's northern beaches. They regularly hung out on or near the beach, and yet over the past few years of growing closer as friends and colleagues, and even spending time at one another's houses, at no point did the subject come up. This common interest lay there, waiting to be unearthed.

Until now. So they conspired to do something truly, fantastically stupid. Why?

Because they were a trifecta of dickheads, that's why.

The following night, still slightly hungover, they assembled close to the international terminal at Circular Quay to execute their daring plan. John had forgotten to dry his suit since his last dive, and as such was the last one to get ready, jamming his lucky legs into his uncooperative wetsuit as the others egged him on.

'Lucky legs?' I quiz Dad.

'Yeah. Lucky they didn't snap off and shoot up my arse,' Dad replies.

I don't know what I expected, but it wasn't that.

At last all three were in their gear. John looked over at his friends, kitted out in full scuba gear, masks, tanks, flippers and all. They looked like idiotic frogs about to pull off some underwater heist. He giggled and gestured towards the water.

Here is what these three toolbags did that night.

First, they walked towards the quay under the cover of darkness, though very likely less subtly than they thought. Next, they scampered out onto the edge of the pier, quickly checked their gear, then leapt in. They had stubby little lights affixed to themselves, which they fumbled at, and suddenly John's world was two idiotic faces, squeezed into scuba masks and pinned behind goggles, lit by tiny golden circles. Silt swam in front of his face. He jerked his thumb, and his two friends followed.

Every once in a while, the *Queen Elizabeth 2* would dock at Circular Quay. The staggeringly vast ocean liner, which cost over £368 million by today's standards, weighed over 70 000 tonnes, and boasted a crew of 1040 and nearly two thousand passengers. It was brimming with artworks and artefacts of great significance, ferried some of the most esteemed politicians, dignitaries and celebrities the world has ever seen, and was a favourite haunt of the royal family. It currently sat berthed, floating quietly like a self-contained city, in the international terminal of Circular Quay. John, Julian and Richie were almost winded by the size and weight of it as they approached from a distance, three hungover specks dwarfed by its planetary bulk.

In order to actually move such a behemoth, you'd need propellers. Big ones. Really big ones. Specifically, two, with five blades each, about twenty feet in diameter.

And on this particular night, three policemen were groggily wending their way along the bottom of the bay towards them.

John shone his light, and sure enough, one of the enormous propellers loomed before them. Above, warped, occasional moving shapes pattered to and fro on the docks, nobody thinking to look down at them — why would they? Who could have guessed anyone would be stupid enough to dive where they were diving? The faint noise of workers heading on and off the great ship filtered down, before being drowned out by the sound of the engine, grinding to life like a leviathan clearing its throat. The rumble became a thick, seismic purr, and every molecule of John's body began to vibrate. Julian's gloved hand gripped John's arm, and he pointed frantically upwards. John shook his head. Richie's hand sluggishly connected with John's arm — slapping someone was, evidently, a great deal harder underwater.

It was leaving soon. They had seconds, John suspected, before the blades would begin to revolve. He cast about, panicking, not entirely sure he'd thought this through as much as he should have, when he saw an enormous pylon. A few metres between the propeller and the quay, his light caught one of the enormous beams of the jetty, and next to it . . .

A rusty, threadbare ladder. The propeller began to move. The three men thrashed and swam like maniacs towards the ladder as fast as their fatigue-addled bodies would allow. Finally, their hands found purchase, and they clung on as tight as they could. And the propeller did what it was designed to do.

It propelled.

John could barely see. Sediment from the ocean floor was being dredged up in huge, harsh gouts, rushing against him and blinding him. The sheer force of the pushback from the waking ocean liner had him clinging to the ladder as if a tornado were trying to tear him off. Richie clung on for another few seconds, then, eyes wide with fear, was hurled backwards into the darkness. Julian held on tight, and shut his eyes.

At last the ship lumbered away into the night, and the sediment around John began to drizzle downwards, sparkling as it did so. He loosened his grip on the ladder, and looked around. Julian was doing the same, and they both scanned the area to see where Richie was. No sign. Julian couldn't say anything to John, but his eyes spoke volumes. They swam back away from the dock and towards a quieter stretch of sandstone wall under cover of darkness.

And there, miraculously, was Richie. He was laughing, and had removed his rebreather. In his hands, clasped above the water like some precious egg, was a very old glass bottle.

'Do either of you clowns know what this is?' he asked, panting.

Dad gets up and heads over to a shelf. He begins rifling through a large book as he talks. 'So, Paul. Hundreds of years back, bottle makers would make amazing bottles for, say, ginger beer. They'd be made from stone, or blown glass and they'd have the makers marks on them. Some were thrown off the wharf, all those years ago and into the water. People thought they were rubbish, shit, so they tossed them.' He leafs through the book, eyes sparkling like Indiana Jones thumbing through his dad's Grail diary, and looks at me.

'And this fucking huge propeller, it just . . .' Dad twirls his fingers in a circle, 'whipped everything up, pulling these things out from way under the sand. Then they'd hang there for a minute before sinking back down. Richie's uncle, he told us, collected these things. Sold them. The one Richie had was worth thousands. So while Julian decided not to keep this hobby up, it became something Richie and I took a little more seriously. Aha! Got it!'

Dad grins, and pulls from the book a slip of very old newspaper.

There, beaming up at me, is a grimy black-and-white photo of my dad, aged 22, alongside Richie, aged 21. They are in Sydney Harbour, in full scuba gear, holding antique bottles. They cling to the side of the harbour wall, and look very pleased with themselves. The headline reads 'COLONIAL TRASH COMES UP CASH'. But they're not at the dock where the *QE2* berthed.

'Why wasn't the photo taken at the pier where the ocean liner actually dredged the shit up?' I ask.

'Because taking the bottles from there was illegal, as was diving underneath the *QE2*. So we said we found them way over on the harbour side. See? This is why you'd have made a terrible cop. Sometimes you gotta . . .' He makes quotation fingers and nods meaningfully.

'Dad, I have no idea what that means.'

'It means bend the truth!'

'No it doesn't. Those are quotation fingers.'

We happily argue for a minute. Hell if he hasn't cheered us both up, though.

38

A-DOOR-ABLE

I'm not able to shake the notion that lying well and being a successful cop are somehow linked. So I push a little. 'Dad, did Julian ever do anything that crossed the line, and not in a playful way?'

He smiles. 'Well . . .'

So Dad launches into a Julian story. A good one. A loose one, certainly . . . but a good one.

John and Julian were coasting along on patrol talking about their dive from a few weeks earlier, when they received a call about a domestic disturbance. One thing to note here: John and Julian bore a special loathing for domestic disturbances. Christine had spent a decent lick of time working with crimes of a sexual nature – in her early years on the force she was the officer North Sydney sent along to the worst of the worst when it came to rapes and abuse. The stories she'd told John and Julian over dinners about Romeo Squad made their toes curl. With Christine now John's wife, a kid on the way and Julian as that kid's godfather-to-be, they had become something of an odd family unit. Perhaps that's why domestics seemed worse to them now than ever before: they felt like a fuck-you to this fantastic new world they were part of.

They pulled up at the apartment block. It was early evening. John straightened his hat, locked the car, and the two officers made their way up to the main entrance. The door had been propped open. Not a great start.

The lift was out, so they climbed the stairs to the third floor.

'What number was it?' Julian asked, scrutinising their surroundings and making a note of everything.

'I don't know. But I think that's it.' John pointed.

The corridor made a hard right about ten metres away, and just before the bend in the hall, a fine white rubble coated the carpet. Rubble? Dust? John squinted. It was certainly something. They made their way towards the mess, and rounded the corner.

The door to what was clearly the source of the domestic call was knocked clean off its hinges. Which is to say, the hinges were still there, twisted almost clear of the doorframe, screws hanging outwards at crazy angles.

'What the fuck happened to the door?' Julian muttered, poking at one of the hinges. Then, just as quickly, his eyes fell on the floor.

The very cheap, very thin door had, it appeared, been pulverised. Reduced to powder. Kicked . . . inwards? Outwards? The scatter pattern of the residue – and there was a shitload of residue, flung onto the carpet, the lino and up the walls – was chaotic. It looked as if someone had kicked the damned thing until it detonated out of its frame.

The crunching of John's and Julian's feet echoed through the place and elicited a faint, stressed 'In here!', which they followed into a living room. Records, clothes and a few indoor plants had been tossed around the place and a chair was tipped over, but the woman sitting cross-legged on the orange couch at the back of the room seemed fine.

Julian went to question her while John checked the rest of the apartment. After a couple of minutes he came back into the room, looking more concerned than ever. 'Do you know who did this, miss?'

'Yeah,' she replied. 'I think he's still around, too.'

This got their attention. Julian was instantly on his feet, alert. He nodded at John, then darted outside to call for backup. John, keeping one eye on the door, made small talk, checking to see if she was hurt. The woman seemed fine, but he saw that her hands were shaking slightly. He shook his head, and turned to Julian, who'd come back inside. 'They're close,' Julian said curtly. 'Should be pulling up now.'

The two officers stood there, facing the door, bracing themselves should the man who had reduced the door to so much dust come back in – god knows they couldn't lock him out. After a moment, John got a call on his radio.

'We got him,' came the tinny voice. 'We got him.'

'Where was he?' John asked, almost immediately regretting his curiosity.

'Behind some scrub, just to the left of the front entrance,' the reply came. John looked over at Julian. They'd walked right past him. John trotted out to the window, and glanced downstairs. Being led away towards another patrol car was one of the biggest men John had ever seen. No neck. Arms like tree trunks.

'Well . . . *that* was close,' he joked nervously. Julian smiled reassuringly at the woman. One of the officers from downstairs came in, tiptoed over the remains of the door, and took over from them, putting her arm around the woman. They both sat down, and she began to take a statement. John and Julian nodded, said their goodbyes, and then headed off.

Dad nods at me, knowingly. 'This,' he says, 'is where the story gets good.'

Pausing for dramatic effect, he leans forward, steepling his fingers. This apparently doesn't make him feel dramatic enough, so he folds his arms instead. 'So. We got back to the station, and filed the paperwork on this brick shithouse. Turns out he was the girl's boyfriend, and he seemed remorseful. I wouldn't want to fuck with him, not after what he did to that door. But he seemed reasonably polite, contrite . . . you know. Well behaved.'

'Now this, Paul, is why this story is important. I only found all of this out later on, from another officer who'd been told this by Julian himself. But here's what I later discovered happened after we knocked off at eleven. Julian and I said goodnight, and I headed off home to look after Christine. Julian got in his car and drove for twenty minutes . . . straight back to the block of flats. He then headed upstairs, up the very same stairs we'd headed up to answer that domestic call.'

He leans back. I can't quite believe where this is going.

'He then entered the apartment – again, from the fucking domestic we'd dealt with hours earlier – and slept with the girl. Now I didn't turn my back on the two of them for more than fifteen seconds, so I fail to see when he could have conveyed to her that he was going to come back, so I can only assume . . . I don't know, that he either knocked on the busted door frame, came in and charmed her into bed, or that they shared some loaded look that contained all of that information. Either way, he fucked her. Then he stayed the night.'

This part clearly has Dad rather pissed. 'Paul, he stayed the night while back at North Sydney, the guy who broke down the door was in custody. But said guy was well behaved, wasn't he? So he got out on fucking bail, at 6 a.m.! So where does he go once he leaves the station? Where does he make a beeline for?'

I'm fairly certain I know the answer already, but I let Dad continue.

'So this hulk steps into the apartment at 7 a.m., or thereabouts, to find his girlfriend in bed with the officer who answered the domestic. The one he watched enter the building from the bushes. But this guy, as we've established, isn't stupid. He might be a piece of shit, but he's not stupid. So he knows he can't bash a cop. So what does he do? In that moment, what does he do?'

Dad lets this hang for a bit.

'See, it turns out Julian didn't change out of his uniform after his shift. Oh no. So piled on the floor at the foot of the bed is Julian's uniform. AND his cuffs. AND his badge. AND his gun. So the caveman thinks, perfect. And in one clean motion, he scoops it up, takes it out to the main room, punches open a window, and flings it out into the garden area. A garden area which not only is overgrown as shit, meaning getting his uniform and gun and so forth is going to take some time, but is facing the street. Then, he storms out.

'Julian wakes up during all of this, and has to run, naked, hands cupping his balls, down into a courtyard facing a main road, cars rushing past on their way to work, grabbing up bits of his police uniform . . . and his gun.'

Dad leans back, angry, exultant, and spent. Never before have I heard my godfather described in such a way, and as the comedy of the visuals ebbs, the variety of lines Julian crossed begin to flare up in my head. 'So . . .' I begin.

Dad barrels on. 'Oh, he never told me, mind you. Never told me. I had to find out from someone else. I don't know, maybe he felt ashamed. He was wound up and went and did something very, very fucking stupid, and dangerous. Do you know what was stopping that man picking up Julian's gun and shooting him dead with it?'

'Nothing,' I reply. 'Absolutely nothing.'

We both sit there, floored.

It's always a curious sensation when you see a little grey in your memories of a stand-up guy.

39

YOU MAY HAVE BEEN A LITTLE PREMATURE

'He was still a great godfather. But . . . oh! Shit. Hang on.'

Dad stands up again, grabs a glass of water, and sits back down. 'A few weeks later, I got a call. Medical emergency. Dropped everything and ran over to the hospital, where Christine was. Oh, sorry, this is the story of how you were born, by the way.'

I find it sort of charming that Dad feels the need to point this out.

'Mum, with you . . . She had what was called toxemia. Really bad. No blood's getting to you, basically. So Mum was about thirty-four weeks, which is six weeks premature. She got rushed to the hospital, and she had this fantastic doctor. I mean, I'm gonna go ahead and assume he's great, given that he drove a Porsche. Rolling in it. Anyway, we went to Royal North Shore and headed into emergency, Mum's there, and the doctor said we need to do an emergency caesarean.'

Mum waves from outside where she's hanging up laundry. I wave back. Something tells me she'd do the specifics of this truer justice than Dad, but I want to see what kind of a picture he paints.

'But as we're there and are being told this, the entire hospital lit up. People running around like maniacs, yelling, barking orders. You see, some major multiple car crash, heaps of fatalities, had just happened nearby, and the call went out to pull staff away to deal with it, meaning all the surgeons and anaesthetists are running off and just . . . left us. So we're sitting there – well, I'm sitting, Mum's lying – and she's in agony. Something very wrong, you're just not waiting like you're supposed to. I was twenty-two at the time. So, so young, Paul. And I know young parents aren't a new or unique thing, but when the doctors finally get back, they tell us they need to give Mum an epidural. Knock her out from the stomach down, inject it into her spine, and I'll have to be up with her top half, holding her hand, talking her through it.

'So they give her the epidural, and we begin. And it's . . . rough. For her, not for me. And I'm holding her hand, and I'm looking into Christine's eyes, and she's staring at the ceiling, concentrating, talking to me, and all I can see for a moment is the train. I'm under the train, and I'm holding another woman's hand as she babbles away, and she couldn't feel her bottom half, either. And I'm there, crying, thinking about that girl's father, and the look on his face as he held that fucking hat in his hands, this country boy, caught the bloody train in for hours to see his daughter, and he was standing there, so polite, so clearly not wanting to be an imposition on us as he asked for directions. And I'm just crying my eyes out, Paul. And Christine is crying. And it suddenly hits me, properly, square between the eyes, that I'm about to be a dad. Me.

At twenty-two. After this whirlwind few years, and all the things I've seen and done, I'm about to have a kid. And then it hits me that I've zoned out and the surgeon is yelling at me. Do I want to come around the other side of the sheet and have a look, she says? So I do.'

Dad blinks hard.

'And they've just cut Mum open, and it's . . . surreal. They just sliced cleanly through all these layers, layer after layer, and then I'm seeing you. Just sort of . . . lying there on top of Mum, inside this kind of container full of fluid. But you had severe toxemia, and when they took you out . . . you were dark blue. Almost black. Pretty much no oxygen. You were so tiny, and . . . I mean, you curled up into the size of a soccer ball, and . . . I was excited. I was so excited. The whole thing was like science fiction, seeing your wife get cut open with a dirty great big blade, and they pull out some blue thing that uncoils and starts screaming, it was like *Alien* for a second there.'

'Cheers, Dad.'

'No worries. And then they gave you a few little tests, the ones they do to gauge how healthy and safe the baby is. True to form for you and your history with exams, you got a three out of ten. Abysmal failure. The Apgar test, I think it's called. Then, before you died on us, they jammed you in a humidicrib, and over the coming week, I'd come visit Mum. And we had a son. You were so small that for the first few weeks after we got you home, we bathed you in this little Tupperware container.'

I'm six foot two, so this image makes me laugh. Dad continues.

'Julian came by the hospital the next day to check on Christine, to meet you, and to give me a cigar he'd bought for the occasion. We smoked them outside. I hate cigars, but it seemed the thing to do. We talked about the birth, and he informed me, more than a little amused, that the shoplifter with the beard and blond hair? The one who stole the gum? Turns out he was a prison escapee. Violent offender, and we, and Woolies, had let him go. "Ah, well," Julian said, "you did this right."

'Julian used to come by the apartment when you were a baby, pick you up and throw you into the air. Probably too high in the air, if I'm honest. Almost level with the ceiling actually. Your eyes used to bug out of your head. In fact in hindsight it probably did you a bit of damage. But you loved Julian, you used to lose your mind when he left.'

This is a lot to take in.

'So, Dad. If you had to sum it up, impart some wisdom to would-be parents reading this . . . what would you say?'

He thinks on this for a good twenty seconds. Finally, he looks at me and simply says:

'It gets better. Much, much later.'

Then he nods, as if he's nailed it.

Maybe he has.

40

LEN: BEATER

To say the birth of his son changed everything for John isn't precisely true. Work continued as normal, his partnership with Julian went on unabated, and his friendships remained the same. It did, however, send him into a brief spiral of contemplative melancholy. He was a dad now. To be crude, he'd been hoping to find solid father figures, and now, shit, he was one. He was a tall, loping 73-kilogram beanpole in an ill-fitting uniform. He'd carried a gun for several years, but only now, with a human being to raise, did he feel truly at risk.

So it was odd, and sad, and terrible when, six months after the birth of his son, he was at the station pulling a late shift when he was approached by Julian. John noticed right away that his friend held in his hand an opened letter. He looked . . . guilty? Confused? John couldn't be sure. He'd not been sleeping much of late —

'You were a noisy little shit, Paul.'
'Still am, Dad.'

— and his intuition was a tad off. 'You get yours yet?' Julian asked, eyes wide. He was jiggling his leg impatiently.

'I don't . . . think so?' John replied. He frowned, stood up, not taking his eye off Julian, and trotted over to his pigeonhole. Inside was an envelope stamped with the New South Wales Police Force emblem, an eagle in flight. He pulled it out, opened it, and read aloud.

'Dear Constable John Verhoeven . . . it is with the greatest respect that we . . . blah blah . . . due to your hard work and . . . mhhm . . . to offer you a . . .'

He looked up at Julian, a huge sheepish grin breaking out over his face.

'These fuckers! They want me to join the detectives! You too, right?'

'Yeah,' replied Julian. They stood there, both a little winded.

John was loving this. The cosmic justice that those bent shitheads would catch wind of him and Julian and their growing arrest record just made this poetic as hell.

'Well . . . no. They can go fuck themselves,' John said to Julian, brandishing the letter.

'You don't think it would be worth thinking over? I mean, I know it pays more. A *lot* more.'

Julian waved the letter, and shrugged. 'You're a dad now, could use the extra income.'

Before John could reply, however, Len Beater yelled for some help.

While John was back at secondary training, he'd heard a confusing rumour. Len Beater had somehow been promoted to supervising sergeant. He and John rarely had cause to interact, true. But Len, perhaps because of the buddy period they'd spent together and the fact that John never blew his cover after the shooting in the park incident, always seemed happy to see him around. It was oddly comforting for John to realise that perhaps he hadn't been saddled with the worst partner of all for his probationary period. Len might be damp and look like a balloon with a face drawn on, but at least he wasn't a bad guy.

The yelling got louder. Julian hung back, while John headed towards the commotion. He rounded the corner to see Len wrestling with a man, easily in his seventies, who was quite clearly catastrophically drunk. John was making his way towards them from behind the wooden counter, and was about to intervene when, seemingly unprovoked, Len raised his steel-toed boot and swung it down in a clean arc towards the old man's leg. There was a sickening crack.

The boot hitting the leg had been obscured by the counter, but John immediately vaulted it, grabbing the arm of the drunken man to hold him up. Len looked frenzied. As John glanced at his old partner, appalled, he could see the whites all the way around Len's irises. His hair had thinned since they'd worked together, and he'd put on decidedly more weight. John could see bags under his eyes. Something wasn't right with the man.

Something was decidedly a great deal worse, however, with the old man who John was now propping up. 'Get him in the cell. Drunk and disorderly, resisting arrest,' barked Len, without making eye contact with John. John yelled over his shoulder. 'An ambo! Call an ambo, now!' He needn't have bothered. Other police were already leaping into action.

The old man woozily spoke through gritted teeth. 'Please,' he slurred. 'My medicine . . . right pocket. Please.' John fumbled inside the man's stinking tweed jacket, until his hand brushed against the contours of a pill bottle. He drew it out, was reading the label, and had just spotted the word 'heart' before Len grabbed the bottle from his hand, opened a window and lobbed it out into the darkness. He then stormed from the room.

Several other officers, who'd not seen the kick but had come running at hearing the old man's agonised cries, converged on John to help get the man somewhere his leg could be looked at. They hauled him down the corridor towards the first aid area, and John watched them go. He was shaking with anger. Julian was nowhere to be seen. Someone rushed past with a first aid kit towards the furor, and John, fuming, headed upstairs to the largely unmanned office area.

Flinging open a boardroom he'd not ever had cause to enter, he headed inside the long, cold space and began to pace back and forth.

You didn't snitch. You didn't. I fucking should, though, he thought. *I didn't technically see the boot hit the leg, but* . . . John had no idea why Len had snapped, but he was furious. Nothing anyone did warranted that kind of violence. But you didn't snitch.

You . . .

Wait.

Wait, he thought. His ears pricked up. He could hear . . .

What the fuck was that?

From beneath his feet, a whispering was issuing forth.

He leaned down, painfully slowly, until he was hunched on all fours on the floorboards of the boardroom. He pressed his ear to the cold surface, and . . .

'I can see you. I'm in here with you. There's no escape. No escape.'

Holy shit, John thought. McKenzie was right.

The building *was* haunted.

And then, as if on cue, John's eyes strayed across to the far corner of the boardroom. There, huddled in the dark, holding a bottle of vodka in one hand and cupping the other around his mouth, and leaning into a heating duct in the wall . . .

Was McKenzie.

The resident 'ghost' of North Sydney station.

John grabbed the drunk spectral visitor by the scruff of his neck, hauled him out of the room, took his bottle and shoved him towards the stairs.

Then John ran outside, and after a few minutes of searching, found what he was looking for. A small bottle of pills. He wiped the bottle down, re-entered the station, and gave them to the battered old man. As he did so, he spotted McKenzie, skulking by the pigeonholes, trying to look busy.

McKenzie went to say something, but thought better of it, and slunk away.

Now *there* was a fuckhead who deserved a kicking.

41

SOMETHING BAD IN STORE

A year passed. A fairly uneventful year, in which John and Julian kept their heads down, Paul was no longer a frightening shade of blue, Christine had returned to health and headed back to work, and things were chugging along smoothly on all fronts. Until one day, over drinks, Christine told John that she was pregnant again.

John was ecstatic. Things took a strange turn, however, when he and Christine were on leave. They'd decided to head down to Warringah Mall with their infant son in a pram, and go record shopping. Well, it started as record shopping. It ended up being them drifting through level after level of David Jones, eyeballing all the things they wanted to buy but probably shouldn't, not if they wanted to be able to feed two kids.

John was having a great day. Life was almost idyllically good. And work was going so well, in fact, that he'd been put forward for a transfer – promotion, really – to forensics. His pathologist friend, the one he'd taken a liking to and who'd shown him the corpse, insisted on writing him a reference and pushed for his application several times. John had not told Julian, but he didn't intend to. He wasn't going to take the job. Things were just right, he thought to himself. You can do so much more good out on the streets. Fuck the detectives and their offer, too. They were better off where they were.

He was thinking this, picturing himself bathed in golden light, saviour of the working man, as he wheeled Paul along with Christine by his side. He was thinking it as he eyed a corduroy jacket. He was thinking it as he lifted the pram up on the escalator, all the while making goo-goo faces at his boy. And he was thinking it still as he made fleeting eye contact with a man coming down the escalator in the opposite direction, descending into the bowels of homewares.

He was a big bastard, with a beard and a quiff of blond hair. A man who, some time ago, had stolen some chewing gum at Woolies in Neutral Bay. A man who had been brought in on charges far worse than shoplifting shortly thereafter.

A man who had escaped prison and who was currently at large.

John told Christine to hold the pram for a bit, and, before he knew what he was doing, yelled, *'Stop! Police!'* The man, clearly remembering John, or at least realising that he was in deep shit, put his head down and tried to act casual.

John, with no badge or gun, pushed past Christine and, legs pumping, yelling 'excuse me' over and over, began shoving his way back down the escalator. He looked, and felt, thoroughly stupid. So he threw caution, and his body, to the wind, and leapt over the partition between the two escalators, coming crashing down on top of the bearded man.

John found himself carried by the man, the two of them staggering down the remainder of the escalator, then picked up and held in the air at a horrible angle. John could smell the man's breath. He briefly considered a witty rejoinder regarding the irony that gum would be helpful at this juncture. But before he could speak, he was unceremoniously heaved skyward, before coming crashing down...

Onto a waterbed.

His attacker looked supremely put out by this.

John sprang up with ease and charged at the man. He then swung his lucky leg right up into the escapee's dick.

The problem with bigger men, John discovered at this exact moment, was padding. With a soft, disappointing *fup*, his foot sank between the hulking man's thighs. The man seized John's leg, yanked it upwards, and sent John slipping backwards in a clean arc, his head connecting with the bed. This time, though, he hit the timber frame, and his vision went dark as pain sang through his neck and spine. He rolled to one side just in time to avoid a size fifteen boot, which came crashing down inches from his face.

By this point, screams had broken out, and shoppers were clearly debating whether to stay or to go. Security had somehow yet to appear. The mania surrounding them, John saw, had momentarily startled the man. By the time the bearded escapee had turned his attention back to his adversary, John was bringing a chair down on the man's back. Sadly, it didn't shatter like in the movies. That's because it's well-made furniture, John thought, filing away a mental note to shop there more often. This note was pelted skyward as a fist drove up into his gut.

John, on the verge of throwing up, leaned on the brute's thigh for support, and, praying his timing wasn't off, snapped his head up, hard and fast. He'd guessed correctly; the man had been hunched over him, likely leering, and the back of John's skull had connected with the man's nose. Pissing blood, the gigantic man reeled back, then, eyes blazing, ran forward, catching John and sending them both crashing through a sideboard that promptly exploded. The two men came skidding to a halt on the lino floor.

The Jam's 'Town Called Malice' tinkled insistently over the PA.

The man was, John saw, straddling him. He woozily stared up as the man, bleeding from the face, beard clotted and eyes wide, raised both fists like hammers. I'm fucked, thought John. I'm proper fucked.

A chair connected with the escapee's head from behind. John looked to see who had swung it, and his heart sank. It was Christine, furious, standing there clutching what appeared to be a replica Eames in her hands.

The man stood up, and before John could move another inch, kicked Christine in the stomach with such force she was propelled across the room.

His pregnant wife.

A second later, a Samoan store security guard the size of a Buick soared through the air and rendered the escapee unconscious.

42

COURT, RED-HANDED

Christine, it should be noted, was fine. More than fine. She hauled herself up at once, and had the security guard not cleaned the escapee's clock she surely would have tried herself. John was bloodied and bruised, but otherwise also OK. Christine pulled him into a standing position and brushed him off.

On patrol the following week, Julian was beyond furious, going on and on that John should have called him. 'Is Chris OK? Did he . . .'

'She's fine,' John assured him. 'Don't think I didn't notice that you didn't ask how I was pulling up.'

'Ahh, it's a split lip, you'll be fine,' Julian replied. 'You need some Dettol? Let me get some Dettol.'

'No!' John barked instinctively. 'No fucking Dettol!'

The very next day, John was called to Manly courthouse, which was where the bearded blond man was being tried for assault. John went in uniform, for maximum effect – not that he was worried the man would get off. This was a prison escapee, after all.

John made his way into the courtroom towards the witness box, a still-bruised 22-year-old. His uniform clung to his body; he caught sight of himself in the mirror on the way in, and understood that looking as young and vulnerable as he did would probably only aid his story further, eliciting a touch more sympathy if nothing else.

He greeted an officer standing by the door and surveyed the room. To his right, with his lawyer, stood the juggernaut whose nose he'd unceremoniously smashed to a fine paste. At the far end of the room sat the judge and various officials. John braced himself, realising he'd have to walk right past the accused, too close for his liking.

As he was about a metre away, the man leaned in slightly and whispered 'fuck you', or something to that effect. John, in that moment, had a choice: shrug it off, or be a bit smug about it.

He chose the latter.

He laughed to himself, quietly smiling at how things had worked out. He was, however, still in 'brace' mode when he caught the faintest whiff of movement in his peripheral vision. He snapped his entire body to one side, and to his shock saw that the escapee was airborne, halfway between his seat and John's throat, his face twisted in a kind of animal fury. Time slowed, and John watched in fascination as two of the police present hurled themselves at the beast, plucking him out of the air like a volleyball. They flung him to the ground and held him there, pinned in place.

The judge, who had stood up and was looking out at the chaos in his courtroom, cleared his throat and came out from behind his bench. He approached John.

'Constable. Would it be safe to assume you feel your life would be in danger if this man were to be let off?'

He then gave John an almost imperceptible nod.

John cottoned on at once.

'Oh. Yes! Yes, I feel my life would be in danger, Your Honour.'

More spitting and swearing from the writhing man behind them perfectly punctuated this moment. The judge smiled at John. 'Right, then. Best put the bastard away, then.'

And that was that.

Only it wasn't. A few days later, John was back at the station busy with some paperwork when he heard his name called. And there, in the corner, was a prisoner, a huge man, being processed before being sent out to Long Bay Gaol.

He began yelling, 'John! John!' But he wasn't bellowing angrily, John noted as he walked over, more than a little tentative. The prisoner had a big dumb grin on his face and he extended his enormous hand. John, baffled, shook it. The man was covered head-to-toe in prison tattoos. But he did look familiar.

'You're Mister Verhoeven's kid, John! How's he doing? Still teaching?'

Then it hit John. John's father, Henk, had been an English teacher for fifty-odd years, largely in rural New South Wales, then on the northern beaches. From somewhere within the recesses of his memory, John recalled this man's face, only far younger, and nestled among a school classroom full of his father's students. He remembered being introduced to that class a long time ago.

And this hardened criminal was standing there, smiling warmly at John. 'Please tell Mr Verhoeven I loved his classes. Just loved them. He got me reading heaps . . . got a lot of time to read lately! Your dad was good to me, mate. A proper teacher. Good bloke. His stuff really had an effect on me.' He paused, and chuckled. 'Right, well clearly not enough of an effect.'

John was somewhat won over. They continued to talk, until the prisoner asked how he got the shiner. John couldn't say exactly why he did it. Maybe it was because he was getting along with the guy, or felt bad for him, or was enjoying talking about his dad, but John told him everything. Told him about the shoplifter, about the gum, about the department store fight, and about the chairs that wouldn't bloody break. About the guy trying to tackle him in the courtroom, and him being tried, and being sent off to Long Bay, too. And then, John finished by telling him that his pregnant wife got hoofed in the stomach by the scumbag.

A look of deadly calm descended over the prisoner's face.

'What was the bloke's name, John?'

And John told him.

He stared at John, who watched some cogs tick over behind his eyes. Finally, he raised his cuffed hands and gave John's shoulder a reassuring pat.

'I'll take care of it, mate.'

Shit, thought John. He went to protest, but the prisoner waved it off as if he were insisting he didn't want seconds. He smiled again.

'Don't sweat it, mate. I'll take care of it.'

And with that, he was whisked away.

And John never saw or heard from either his father's ex-student or the chewing gum escapee again.

'Fucking hold on a second, Dad,' I protest. 'Did you get this piece of shit killed? Did you get someone shanked, or not?'

Dad shrugs. 'I have no idea, Paul. I have no idea.'

43

A VALIANT EFFORT

John still occasionally harboured desires to be a detective. They bubbled up whenever he and Julian would crack a particularly tough case, or, you know, do detective work while on duty. John had politely turned them down, but he kept the letter in his desk. They continued reaching out every once in a while, but he'd resolved to stay where he was with Julian. Julian assured John he'd told them where to stick it, and that the detectives continued knocking at his door. In spite of this, they both still acknowledged it'd be nice to say yes, while agreeing firmly that they'd just end up becoming as warped as all the rest. But whatever urge John had left was about to swiftly dissipate.

There was a certain hierarchy to the cars: 6-1 was the wagon, and was for the hard stuff; 6-2 was one step down. And 6-3? This one was for support. It was also, typically, a Valiant. A dangerous car in a pursuit because if you tried to pull a hairpin turn it could veer wildly off the road. If patrol cars were Thunderbirds, the Valiant was the shit one. Thunderbird 5.

One night, John and Julian were given 6-3. The Valiant. The one with the vinyl roof, like the cheap couch John's brother would pass out on from time to time. They exchanged a look and made their way over to do their checks. That morning there'd been a rash of bag snatchings reported by elderly ladies. John hated bag snatchers. What he'd discovered was this: a bag snatching was, if the snatchee was pliant, relatively harmless in the grand scheme of things. But pliant was the key word here. Old women are tough. And they regularly held on to their bags.

As they drove around that morning, the radio painted a horrible picture. A gang of five, two women, three men, all in their late teens, had spent hours snatching bags from across several suburbs. As John and Julian drove, listening intently for any leads, the report came through. A ninety-year-old woman had been standing at a set of traffic lights at a busy intersection. The snatchers had grabbed her bag, and, a World War II survivor, this woman rightfully planted her feet and said, according to a nearby witness, 'Not bloody likely.' And when an unstoppable force meets an immovable object, something's, as the song goes, gotta give.

The woman hung on tight as they dragged her, and her bag, across the road and into traffic.

Eventually she let go, but not, as the radio informed them, before she'd been seriously injured. She'd fallen hard, her hip had fractured, and she lay on the road as the bag snatchers fled the scene.

John and Julian, both on the warpath, made their way towards the scene hoping to catch some whiff of a clue. Sadly, though, the radio gave them a dispiriting update as far as their need for vengeance was concerned. Two of the bag snatchers had just been caught out of area, and were being taken to North Sydney for lockup. The other three had disappeared without a trace, and their car, which at this point would be laden with dozens of stolen bags all linking them to their crimes, was in the wind. And what's more, John and Julian were in the car assigned to menial duties, mainly reported prangs. Today, this case wasn't in their wheelhouse. There was nothing they could do.

'Fuck this!' exclaimed John. He nodded at Julian, and Julian nodded back.

'Fuck this,' Julian agreed.

Back at the station, the place was in meltdown. There'd been a spate of serious prangs that morning, and police were running back and forth. Phones were ringing off the hook. John fronted the nearest senior friendly face he could find: Harding's.

'Morning, boys! What can I do you for?' It would have sounded clichéd coming from anyone else, but spilling from Harding's lips it sounded completely sincere. Honest. So John answered just as honestly.

'Sir, we're hoping to see the prisoners. Bag snatchers. Two males, late teens, would have been brought in —'

Before he could finish, Harding tutted, not unkindly. 'John, John. They're in lockup, but it's not for you to sort out . . . Go and have a look if you want, but that's it. They're in the big one.' 'The Big One': the group cell where prisoners are corralled until the police know just what to do with them. Raising an eyebrow, Harding gave John and Julian a gentle 'shoo', and got back to his paperwork.

When John and Julian were halfway down the corridor towards the Big One where the two bag snatchers now resided, an idea hit John.

Harding was right. It wasn't for them to sort out. And for that matter, what could two young cops find out that the detectives couldn't when they rocked up later that morning to take custody? This wasn't going to achieve anything. A cop couldn't fix this.

John bolted to the locker room and changed into jeans and a white t-shirt. Two minutes later he ran back into the corridor, caught his breath, and told Julian to cuff him.

Julian's eyebrows almost shot off. 'What? Are you out of your fucking mind?'

Perhaps he was. But it was a little late to back out now. 'It's fine, we just need to hurry this up. Cuff me, take me in. Give me ten minutes. Then, call me back, cuff me back up, and get me out.' Julian processed this and glanced over his shoulder. No other cops were around. Eventually, he made a reluctant whining noise, grunted, and pulled out his cuffs. The con was on.

As John rounded the corner, a few things became apparent. First of all, he wasn't wearing any shoes; in his rush to get changed he'd decided not to put them on, and was now regretting that decision. Secondly, the huge cell was relatively empty. A drunk was asleep in a corner and against the back wall, sitting together and whispering angrily, were the two purse snatchers. One was monstrously ugly while the other was unfeasibly handsome. John didn't make eye contact as Julian, who'd grabbed the keys without anyone noticing, tried to still his shaking hands and open the door. John went inside, and turned his back to the cell, putting his hands through the bars to have his cuffs removed. He could hear the two suspects go quiet behind him.

He was in the shit now.

Julian locked the door, gave him the briefest of looks, and walked back down the corridor.

And there was John. No shoes, no badge, no gun, locked in a cell with two criminals, and a drunk. He moved to a bench across from the two, gave them a curt nod, and folded his arms as if to go to sleep.

'I don't remember exactly what happened next, but I think I can dredge up most of the key beats. OK? Right. First, I remember the adrenaline. I was sitting right next to the two crim scumbags. These were bad blokes. And if anyone in the station came by and saw me . . . I'd be fucked. That's what I figured out as Julian walked away . . . I was fucked. I'd be fired if I was found impersonating a prisoner for information that could be inadmissible in court. But I wasn't going to hurt anyone, and I wasn't accepting a bribe, or planting evidence or anything like that. The only person at risk here was me. And if I could find out anything, *anything*, to put these guys away, anything legit . . . look. I just had to find the car. So I sat there.'

I hold my tongue.

'I sat there and listened, and sure enough, they began talking about some car. And I perked up, and told them, 'Oh! Shit! I think I lifted one of those once.' And they gave me this look, and I thought for a second I was fucked, but they eventually asked what I was in there for. And I said a break and enter, but I preferred cars. I loved cars. So, we're sitting there, and we're talking about cars, and eventually, I realise my time is almost up. And I look over at the wall adjoining the corridor, and I can see a tuft of hair round the corner, and I realise Julian must be back there on all fours, listening. So I pull the trigger.'

'"So ... what do you fellas drive?"'

The two criminals fixed John with a truly harrowing look, and instantly John knew he'd gone too far. He'd fucked it. He was readying himself to make a bolt for the gate when the leader of the two, the handsome one, looked up at John and smiled.

'Cortina. Tan piece of shit, white seats. Gotta get something new one of these days.'

Then he turned back to his friend and continued chatting. John exhaled. There was so much adrenaline surging through him he could feel a thumping in his skull, and he became suddenly nauseous. And before he could process what to do next, Julian was at the gate, gruffly waving John over. 'You,' he barked. John got up as calmly as he could, mumbled something about his lawyer finally having called, and swore at Julian. He popped his shaking hands through the bars, was re-cuffed, let out, led around the corner and taken quickly to the locker room. Mercifully it was empty, and after the cuffs were removed, John collapsed on the floor. He realised he hadn't blinked the entire time.

Once John was back in uniform, they thanked their lucky stars that an all-cars bulletin hadn't exposed the fact that they were off the map for a full half-hour. They quickly headed back to the car. And that's when they saw it. Two detectives leaving the station with the ringleader. The adonis. They watched as the group made their way over to Babcock House, the monolith that housed Detective HQ.

And John, wanting to properly cap off his caper by watching it get closed up, told Julian to follow him. So they walked over to Babcock House – a building neither of them felt particularly well disposed towards – and hung by the entrance for a good ten minutes. Then, having let enough time pass, they headed upstairs. They made their way to the main floor, and after asking for directions in roundabout ways, headed towards the interrogation rooms. Julian waited and John approached the window of the nearest room.

John saw the bag snatcher inside. Both detectives had their backs to him, but the bag snatcher saw John. And John watched as the terrible realisation of what he'd done appeared on his face. Before John could relish his accomplishment, his brain inventoried the entire room. One of the detectives held the sawn-off handle of a pool cue, with a hole in the end and a leather thong strung through to serve as a makeshift handle. It looked like a jury-rigged nightstick. John also registered that the suspect was shirtless, his stomach covered in fresh welts. And as the look of recognition faded on the bag snatcher's face, the handle came crashing into his stomach. John, watching for a reaction, watching for a cry of pain, saw nothing at all. The man didn't react. And John felt sick.

Any faint hopes he'd had about being a detective were now in the wind.

John and Julian, however, agreed upon one thing: the guy wasn't going to talk. He was made of sterner stuff. So they hightailed it out of Babcock House and drove, simmering the entire time, towards where the initial arrest had been made. They swept the nearby streets until they found a tan Cortina. The boot was unlocked, and it was full of stolen purses. John called Harding to tell him the good news. When asked how they'd stumbled upon such a find, he simply paused and replied 'it was for us to sort out'. Harding chuckled.

'So,' said Julian as they sat in 6-3 together, waiting for backup to arrive. 'That plan. To have me march you into the cell in cuffs pretending to be a prisoner. Where'd you come up with that?'

And without missing a beat, John replied.

'*Star Wars.*'

44

THE HOUSE ON THE HILL

I hit pause and run off to the bathroom. And when I return, there it is, sitting on the table.

The photo.

The second of the two. Scorch marks on a wooden floor, matted hair, blood.

I feel a wave of something between nausea and embarrassment at being nauseated.

'Paul. The reason I've told you so much, why I've gone into so much detail, is because I want you to have context,' Dad says. 'So . . . I guess we'd better get it over with.' He stares at me and I swear something passes across his eyes. He doesn't want to be talking about this. That much is clear.

He does, though.

He sure as shit does.

John had woken up with an odd feeling in the back of his skull, thinking that something was off. He couldn't quite place it, but it had been building for a while now. He was preoccupied, mulling this over, and trying to use his tongue to fish something out of his teeth after lunch, when the call came. Julian answered. Somerset Street, Mosman. The fire brigade had been called to put out a small fire in the driveway of a home. Why were the cops being called? Julian asked. Because the object on fire was a bucket, VKG said. Full of clothes. Bloody clothes. Julian nodded, and off they went.

They pulled up outside the house at about 4 p.m. The low-cloud cover meant that it was already uncommonly dark. The street was deadly quiet, apart from the sounds of a dog barking a few houses over. A huge oak tree, one of the biggest John had ever seen, jutted out of the front yard of the house, branches shifting ever so slightly. And there, sitting in the driveway, was a large bucket, charred black, full of what used to be bloody clothes. John and Julian exited the car and approached the bucket from either side, sizing it up. Julian popped a pair of surgical gloves from his belt and drew them on. He leaned down and gingerly prodded the bucket, then tilted it to one side. The burns had melted clean through one end. He turned to John, looking grim.

'There's a hole in the bucket, dear Henry.'

John exhaled and crouched down, too. The clothes were so badly burned that any hint of what they'd once been was well and truly scorched into oblivion, but he thought he saw a name tag. He looked closer. It was completely illegible now. The wind picked up, and the tree made slow, undulating motions, like an ocean just out of reach above their heads. They stood as one, nodded at one another, and headed down towards the house.

As they approached the door, John noticed it was ajar. He nodded at Julian. Julian nodded back. John nudged the door open with his foot, and they headed inside, guns drawn.

The first thing that struck John was the smell. That, and the house didn't seem quite right. He caught on to how stupid that sounded as he muttered it to himself, but there was something palpably wrong with this place. For one thing, all the blinds were drawn. They were a yellowy gauzy fabric, which meant that the light filtering in looked sickly. Jaundiced. John sniffed the air. There it was again. The smell of something burning, along with . . . Something he couldn't quite place. Something else.

'John.' Julian had wandered off to the left and into the kitchen. John crested the corner, and came to a halt behind his partner, who was standing there, jaw slack, gun by his side. John followed his gaze. He saw, stacked haphazardly on the counter and the five shelves above it, hundreds upon hundreds of jars of varying sizes. He craned his head closer for a better look, and almost wished he hadn't. Preserved frogs, dead birds, and a staggering array of fetuses of indeterminate animals. The room was filled with the smell of brine, mingled with embalming fluid. And blood. Julian covered his mouth, and turned to John, all humour gone from his face.

'This is fucked, mate.'

John nodded in response. They exited the kitchen, guns up and ready.

John was still in something of a daze from the fumes in the kitchen when he spotted, on the far wall, what appeared to be a human silhouette. He beckoned Julian over. They stared at the shape on the wall, trying to figure out what it was, before finally, Julian's face fell.

'It's like fucking Hiroshima.'

John took a few steps back and took it all in. Julian was right. Etched on the wall, seared there in a pose of what appeared to be ecstasy, arms aimed skyward and head thrown back, was the clear, terrible outline of a woman, ringed in ash. Julian tapped John's shoulder, then spun him around; another, equally contorted image lay across the room. Then another in the hallway, seeming to lead them further into the depths of the house.

John felt his blood go cold. He felt sick, and slow, and it took everything in him not to run outside and back to the car.

Julian spoke up, barely above a whisper. 'I'll take the bedroom, you take the bathroom.'

John nodded slowly. The fumes were making his eyes burn. He watched as Julian inched his way into the darkness of the hallway while he ducked into the tiny bathroom, knuckles now white around the handle of his revolver.

The sink was ringed with an array of candles, all burnt down to the quick. Most had guttered out, but a few still cast light about the place. He stepped on something small and hard, and bent down, pulling out his flashlight. He turned it on and shone it upon the object in his hand.

A human molar.

John dropped it and stood up in shock, his flashlight catching the sink.

He told himself to stay calm, reminding himself what the fuck his job was. He took a deep breath to steel himself, and caught that smell again. He checked the sink to see if the smell was in fact coming from there, and instead found more teeth. Six of them, clotted with great, heaping gobs of thick black blood.

'Well, fuck,' John breathed, pulling back.

His flashlight swung around across the small room to reveal blackened silhouettes of handprints on either side of the mirror. He made a mental note of this, suppressed the urge to vomit, and backed out of the hellish room.

'John! John, get the fuck down here,' came Julian's now decidedly less-than-composed call from deeper inside the house.

John, in no hurry to stay by himself any longer, darted down the hallway, and found himself in what appeared to be the master bedroom.

He surveyed the scene and resisted an old, familiar urge to cross himself.

There was something off in this room, too, but more so than the rest of the house.

In the centre of the room on the floor there was a mass of blood. Burnt fragments of hair and skin clung to the floorboards. John's eyes fell on two warped, melted impressions in the centre of the mess. Clearly seared into the floorboards were two buttock and thigh marks. Burnt flesh clung in tattered filaments to the grooves of the wood. Blood and shit was everywhere. The smell of petrol filled the room. Julian gagged.

The bed, too, was utterly ruined. Blackened, wet with viscera, urine, blood, everything.

John's eyes followed the trail of gore from the bed to the grooves in the centre of the room. He then traced with his finger the burnt silhouettes seared into the wall as they kaleidoscoped along and back out into the hallway. When he turned back to the bed, Julian, his gloves still on, had picked up a large, serrated kitchen knife off the bedspread. Blood caked its blade, and Julian gingerly put it back down.

They looked at each other, looked around at the room, and then they got the fuck out of there.

Once they were outside, the house still felt deeply wrong, but at least they weren't in it, John reasoned. He and Julian ducked back up to the car and radioed back to command.

'See,' says Dad, somewhat paler than normal, 'our shift was going to end soon. So we were going to have to hand this one off to someone else to get the credit. But Paul, you know what kind of cops we were. So, we radioed our boss, and explained to him, in hushed voices, exactly what we'd found. And in an incredible moment, our old mate Harding paused, then said he'd fucking had it with detectives in his area sweeping up the good cases. So right then and there, he authorised overtime for the two of us. We had as much time as we needed, within reason. But before he hung up, he told us he'd call in backup from our station, on the QT, to cordon off the scene. He said we'd need that, because there was something up at the hospital we had to see. And fast.'

John and Julian pulled up to Royal North Shore Hospital, right up to the very entrance where months earlier, John had rushed in to see the birth of his son. And as they coasted into the emergency bay they saw a small blue hatchback, parked at an odd angle, occupying two parking spots. John looked at Julian, and they immediately stopped the car. They bolted over to investigate.

The driver's door was open. The smell of cooked blood filled the cabin. The white leather seat was blackened and melted, and fused to it were two very familiar impressions. Skin from two charred hands clung to the wheel, and blood pooled around the pedals.

John and Julian wasted no time sprinting into the hospital. It didn't take long to find out where she'd ended up.

Within minutes they had entered a room where the woman lay under foil blankets, her blackened face peering out. An older man stood in the corner, watching. The head nurse leaned in and told them what had happened, as best as she could manage given how hard she was struggling with what she'd seen. About thirty minutes earlier the woman had pulled up, still on fire, bleeding from two deep saw-marks on her wrists.

'The knife,' sighed Julian. John nodded.

The nurse went on to explain this woman had third-degree burns to 98 per cent of her body, the exception being the soles of her feet. 'I swear,' she choked, stumbling on her own words for an instant before continuing, 'the sliding doors opened, and there was a naked woman stumbling towards me. Her skin was falling off in handfuls. She was hunched over. I . . .' The nurse trailed off.

John looked up again at the old man standing across the room, off to one side, pale as a sheet. He clutched a small canvas bag to his chest, clearly in shock, and was watching the barely breathing woman with a heartbreaking look that John immediately recognised.

He was her father.

'He was a retired police officer, he told us. An ex-sergeant. And he told us she was a witch.'

I see that strange something cross Dad's eyes again.

'We're all standing there, consoling this poor man who'd gotten a call to come and be with his daughter as she died, and I'm slowly realising that we're only a few rooms from where you were born.

'So,' Dad says slowly, 'just as I'm processing that, something extraordinary happens. Out of nowhere, the woman pulled free of the blankets, sat violently upright, looked right at us, suddenly totally lucid, and in a clear voice, said her last words.'

'What were they?' I ask.

'"I have been cleansed."'

Dad wipes tears from his eyes. He suddenly looks much older than he had minutes prior.

'And then she died. And that was it.'

We sit there, facing one another. I look down at the photo, then back up at Dad. After a minute or so, I think I know what I want to say to him.

'Dad, two questions. First . . . do you think she was a witch?'

'Maybe. She certainly thought so. She was trying to get something out of her, and she killed herself in the process.'

I let that sink in. Time for my final question. 'Did you have dreams about this, like I did?'

This time he does hesitate. Then, looking me dead in the eyes, he says simply, 'I still do sometimes.'

45

BACK AT THE START

It was ten on a Saturday night. A small, dented car thrummed across the Sydney Harbour Bridge.

John checked the fuel gauge on his shitbox Holden. A little while back, he'd taken a punt and obtained it at a police auction. The car used to belong to a low-level dealer and as such came with fluoro fuzzy dice, dangling idiotically like two brazen cuboid testicles from his rear-view mirror. He kept them on, though. He'd grown kind of attached to them.

John flicked the dashboard, silently coaxing the car to hold out just a little longer. He had just enough fuel to make it across town. He stretched, sighed deeply, and checked his mirror.

He was being followed.

Which is to say he was being tailgated. Enthusiastically. A tan convertible, housing three tattooed men shouting and jeering, veered left and right, edging closer and closer to the fender of John's Holden. John started sweating bullets. It was easily thirty degrees outside, and he was stubbornly clad neck to waist in a thick navy blue sweater his wife had knitted for him. He wiped his brow and impatiently waved them past, suppressing the urge to pump on the brakes. But they chose to forgo this opportunity and continued their game of 'not touching you, you can't get mad' for another five city blocks.

Finally, their car coasted to a halt next to John's at the lights out front of the George Street cinemas. The marquee read 'Puberty Blues', the letters flickering in time with John's twitching eyelid. He wound down his window, and slowly turned to face the three gentlemen who'd been either harassing or wooing him for the last ten minutes. In either case they now had his undivided attention. An upbeat disco track coursed from their speakers.

All three had close-set eyes. And as they continued yelling and making menacing gestures, the biggest of the three, sitting in the driver's side passenger's seat, yelled, 'Nice car, dickhead.' He then punctuated his remark by flinging a crumpled VB can directly at John. The can pinged off John's forehead, and fell with a clatter onto the road.

John had spent a lick of time trying to process the single most disturbing series of events in his entire life. He'd watched a witch die. He'd tried to comfort her father. He had a kid of his own at home, and had spent the better part of six months dodging a litany of cases which, through some confluence of bad luck, dealt almost exclusively with dead children and grieving parents. And John, remembering all of this, and perhaps not entirely in control of his critical faculties given the heat, the jeering and the small stinging welt on his forehead, calmly reached down and unclipped his holster.

In one swift movement his arm snapped out of the window, fully extended, with his gun aimed directly at the forehead of the driver of the convertible. The lights stayed red. All three men in the car next to John froze, staring at him as he held the gun quite steady, arm outstretched, bridging the gap between the two cars like a woollen pylon.

And then, the lights turned green. John withdrew his gun, holstered it, nodded politely at the trio and pulled away into the night. After driving half a block, he pushed aside the fluffy dice and looked into his rear-view mirror. The convertible had yet to move. Three cars were banked up behind it, impatiently honking their horns. John smiled, patted the dashboard reassuringly, and drove away. And he thought about what Len Beater would have done, or what some bent detective would have done.

But John wasn't that kind of cop.

He wasn't *that* loose.

EPILOGUE: IT'S OVER

Dad sits for a minute before continuing. 'Do you want to know why I wanted to explain everything to you before the witch story?'

I shrug.

'Because the witch wasn't why I found that day so unsettling, although I absolutely did. I still do. It's because when Julian and I headed outside, after we'd watched that woman die, and tried to console her father, we walked out of the hospital. We stood for a minute in the car park where we smoked those cigars after you were born. And in that moment, my best friend stopped me, and told me, "They asked again. I took the transfer. I'm going to be a detective." It knocked the wind out of me . . . I thought we understood each other.

'And I suppose in a way we did, because we stayed friends, for a while longer, at least. But we weren't partners any more. We weren't a unit like we were up until that point. Not any more. So I gave him half-hearted congratulations, I think. I don't exactly remember how I reacted. And the next day, I got back in touch with forensics. Thankfully they still wanted me. Looking back on it, I know why I felt a pull towards it – it was that first time I saw a dead body.

It stuck with me, and I wanted to understand it. So I kept pushing, like you did with me today. I kept diving deeper to try and understand it better. Being a detective would never have allowed me to see the things I saw, and learn what I learned in forensics.'

I'm stunned. 'So . . . Is *this* why you and Julian don't talk any more?'

'It was the *beginning* of why, yes. But look, I know you wanted a story from me about me and Julian.'

My head is swimming a little. 'Dad, I don't get it. I heard you talking about the things he did in roundabout ways, and I thought . . .'

'Paul, I complained about him because we drifted apart years later and because I was sad we drifted apart. People change. There's no big twist there, that's just what happens sometimes. You're a storyteller. I think you spent years telling yourself certain things, and adding bits to a story about Julian making some dramatic heel turn. Paul, mate . . . I know you wanted a buddy cop story about me and your godfather. But for me, this wasn't ever really about a partner, or *the* partner. It was about me trying different partners on, seeing who fit. Seeing who didn't fit. Seeing . . . you know, who fit for a while until they . . .'

'Fucked you over?'

Dad laughs. He stands and stretches, cracking his back with a series of emphatic pops. 'He didn't fuck me over. I mean, he took the transfer, but that's OK. You wanted to know why you didn't end up like me, and why you weren't . . .'

He half points to himself, making a 'like . . . all of *this*' sort of gesture, and shrugs.

'Paul, look. I'm glad you didn't see the things I did. People aren't meant to see that shit. You're different, and that's good, mate.

That's so, so good. You weren't meant to do what I did or be like I am. You've turned out great, and you didn't have to go through what I did to turn out that way. As for the photos . . . it was a horrible case. Would have upset anyone, simple as that. You're no weaker than anyone else for letting it get to you. It got to me, too, all right? But I hope you can see that you barely had a taste. I copped the whole thing.'

I think on this. 'But . . . knowing about the witch, why do you think this one photo reached out, grabbed my subconscious, and worked me up so badly?'

Dad threw his hands up. 'Because she was a witch!'

'You really think she was a witch?'

'Well, fuck! Probably! I don't know!'

We sit there for some time, silent, utterly spent.

'Listen,' says Dad. 'All of this stuff was child's play compared to forensics. This was a fucking appetiser, mate. Forensics will ruin you, if you've got the stomach for it. Think you can handle it?'

I smile. If he could live through it, the least I can do is listen to the next part of his story, to try to learn something.

'Your mum, she's a proper partner. She's perfect. We work so well together. You know? And . . . You, you're a good partner, too, Paul.' And then, after a pause, he smiles. 'I actually think you'd have made a decent cop.'

'Really?' I say, eyes widening.

'Fuck no, mate,' he chuckles, standing up to leave. He turns before heading out the door.

'Fuck no.'

ACKNOWLEDGEMENTS

There's quite a few people to thank, because there's no way I could have written this without help.

I'd like to thank the wonderful folks at Penguin Random House for being so, so patient with me, especially my editor, Cate Blake, who picked up *Loose Units* in the first place. They're a scrappy, can-do, up-and-coming publishing house and I'm sure we'll be hearing more from them in the near future.

I should also thank the superbly talented Marieke Hardy for taking a chance on me by putting me on Triple J Breakfast, then for shunting me under the nose of Penguin. Melanie Ostell for copy-editing this seething mass of words. Oh! My grandmother Margaret, who basically taught me to read. And speaking of teaching, Mr Staker, Mr Walsh, Ms Derwent, Mr Buckley, Jodi Brooks, Ben Peek . . . teachers so good they re-forged my brain into something nearing functional. And to all the others whose names I've forgotten.

Except for the maths teachers. They know what they did.

There's all my friends who lent an ear and talked me through all the crises associated with writing a book, my very supportive family, Rove, Ben Law and others who I'm sure I'm forgetting.

Like my dad, *Loose Units* is a mish-mash of contradictions, of genres, of experiences. Dad's very easily distracted, and so am I. The fact that I was able to pin down his fluttering, skittering brain and siphon out enough to build a somewhat labyrinthine crime novel should show you how much I've enjoyed, and cared about, this endeavour. I really have had a white-hot ride writing this book, and it's been more rewarding than anything I've ever done creatively before. And apart from Penguin saying no to a scratch-and-sniff foldout in the middle, there've been no roadblocks. This story has been unfathomably fun to write.

But do you want to hear the best part? There are so many more stories to come.

See you soon.